MASTER PRODUCTION SCHEDULE PLANNING

MASTER PRODUCTION SCHEDULE PLANNING

Robert A. Gessner

A Wiley-Interscience Publication

John Wiley & Sons

New York   Chichester   Brisbane   Toronto   Singapore

Library of Congress Cataloging in Publication Data:

Gessner, Robert A.
  Master production schedule planning.

  "A Wiley-Interscience publication."
  Includes index.
  1. Scheduling (Management)   I. Title.

TS157.5.G47   1985   658.5'3   85-12229
ISBN 0-471-82658-8

Printed in the United States of America

10 9 8 7 6 5 4 3 2 1

PREFACE

The novice, the master scheduler, the production planner, and the company executive will find *Master Production Schedule Planning* to be an educational tool.

This type of planning is the key to effective control within manufacturing. The proper selection of alternate techniques can turn a potential MPSP system failure into a success. To this end, the book addresses why MPSP functions are performed and the pros and cons of the various techniques that can be used to perform those functions.

Some of the major topics discussed include:

Defining master production schedule planning

Business planning and forecast data management considerations

Master production planning

Resource planning

This book will have a significant impact in the following areas:

Manufacturing companies (both job shop and repetitive)

    Production planners

    Master schedulers

    Executives

Consulting firms that teach and install manufacturing systems

Colleges and universities that teach manufacturing

Computer software firms that produce manufacturing software

As the manufacturing industry shifts toward the repetitive environment, MPSP becomes the significant application for effective management. This book provides the necessary information for proper understanding and installation of an MPSP system.

ROBERT A. GESSNER

Kennesaw, Georgia
September 1985

CONTENTS

PART ONE.   DEFINING MASTER PRODUCTION SCHEDULE
            PLANNING

Introduction to MPSP   **3**
Everyone Is Doing It   3
MPSP Functions and How They Relate   5
Who Needs MPSP   12

2. **An Overview of MPSP Functions**   **15**
Demand Analysis Planning   15
Master Production Planning   21
Master Schedule Planning   25
Resource Planning   28

PART TWO.   BUSINESS PLANNING AND FORECAST DATA
            MANAGEMENT CONSIDERATIONS

3. **A Make-to-Stock and Package-to-Order Company**   **33**
The Family Concept   33
The Environment of the Make-to-Stock Company   35
An Analysis of the Previous Year's Sales Activity   39
Estimating the Sales for the Future Year's Activity   42
Conversion of Sales Dollars to Unit Quantities   45
Building the Forecast   49

4. **A Make-to-Order Company**   **55**
The Environment of the Make-to-Order Company   55
An Analysis of the Previous Year's Sales Activity   57
Developing the Projections for the Future Year   58

PART THREE.   MASTER PRODUCTION PLANNING (MPP)

5. General MPP Philosophies and Considerations   69
    Differing Philosophies   69
    Bucket Size Considerations   70
    Multiple Plan Considerations   76
    CMLT Time Fence Considerations   78
    Input Data Blending Considerations   78

6. Product Family Aggregation   85
    Determining How Items Fit Into a Family   85
    Aggregation Data   91

7. Product Family and Item Plan Management   95
    The Basic Plan Management Logic   95
    Family Plan Management   114
    Item Plan Management   115
    Comparison Displays   116

PART FOUR.   MASTER SCHEDULE PLANNING (MSP)

8. General MSP Philosophies   121
    Plan Via MPP, Via MSP, or Via Both   121
    MSP Demand   122
    Conversion—Buckets and Quantities   123
    Possible MSP Displays   131

PART FIVE.   RESOURCE PLANNING

9. Building an Item Resource Profile   137
    Some Basic Definitions   137
    A Simple Item Profile   138
    The Composite Item Profile   141

10. Building a Family Resource Profile   153
    Item Profile Mix Percentages in the Family   153
    What is a Family Profile?   155
    Summary   163

APPENDIXES

  I. Where MPSP Fits Within the Functions of a Typical Industrial
      Sector Company   165

  II. Testing the Disaggregation of Product Families Using Mix
      Percentages   175

 III. Glossary of Terms   199

 IV. Conversion of Sales Data to Manufacturing Data   213

PART ONE

DEFINING MASTER PRODUCTION SCHEDULE PLANNING

CHAPTER ONE

INTRODUCTION TO MPSP

EVERYONE IS DOING IT

The title to this section implies that everyone is doing Master Production Schedule Planning (MPSP). To a certain degree that is true—everyone is doing something they consider to be MPSP!

Company A states, "We use an adjusted production forecast that we convert into firm planned orders for input to MRP (Material Requirements Planning)."

Company B says, "We create a product supply plan from business planning. We match the plan against projected sales to determine when we need to schedule the release and receipt of orders."

Company C feels they do it right. "We build 348 products, but the key assemblies that go into those products are built on three main assembly (flow) lines. Therefore, we explode those 348 products to the key assembly level and then aggregate the quantities into product groups, which are used to develop weekly build schedules."

Company D says they do MPSP without a computer. "We have only four models. We have a lot of options on those four models, but they are easy to plan. We use a magnetic board on the wall. Our chief planner lays in the ship date, figures offsets and lays in the option start dates (keeping shop capacities in mind), and finally, figures offsets and lays in when key materials should be ordered."

Possibly you are starting to understand a main MPSP problem. Given 20 different companies, 20 different varieties of MPSP will exist, each company using their own terms to define what they do and each performing different functions according to their needs.

The functions that may or may not be identified as part of MPSP are often described as:

Demand management (which often includes Forecasting and Order Entry)
Demand analysis
Final assembly scheduling
Production planning
Forecasting
Customer order servicing (which usually includes Order Entry)
Order entry
Master production planning
Master production scheduling
Master schedule planning
Resource planning
Rough-cut capacity planning
Plant (flow line) scheduling
Resource requirements planning

It is apparent that some of the above-named functions describe the same thing. It is also obvious that there are conflicting opinions as to the functions that actually constitute MPSP.

This confusion in terminology is partly due to the evolution of MPSP concepts. A manufacturing company that did not utilize forecasting when they decided to implement MPSP might naturally consider forecasting to be part of their new MPSP system. Conversely, a company that had a computer-based statistical forecasting system in place when the decision was made to implement MPSP would probably consider forecasting to be outside of the scope of MPSP.

As to what terminology was applied to functions (and data), these varied by what the particular user felt was comfortable. One company feels that the term "production planning" applies to a gross level of planning across a three-year horizon at a family planning level. Another company feels that "production planning" is defined as what the production control manager does in the development of a daily production schedule.

The purposes of this book are to explain what MPSP is, how it can function, and to describe some potential pitfalls that an MPSP user should be aware of. To accomplish this objective, some standards are defined for the identification of functions and data elements within this text.

As you proceed through the text, you will learn that there is no universal best way to perform MPSP that applies to all companies. There is, however, a way for each specific company to understand the best way for them—by being aware of the available design alternatives.

The following sections use many examples to illustrate various approaches of MPSP, as the discussion flows through the functional areas of MPSP in a logical sequence.

MPSP FUNCTIONS AND HOW THEY RELATE

As described in the preceding section, there is a large amount of confusion as to what functions (or subfunctions) relate to MPSP. Two approaches are used in this text to provide you with some understanding of manufacturing functional relationships.

Appendix I is titled, "Where MPSP Fits Within the Functions of a Typical Industrial Sector Company." This appendix structures about 248 potential applications into where they would most logically fit in a typical industrial-sector company. The structure is based on major business areas, since a company does not normally structure its organization based on application areas. This causes confusion when we attempt to identify necessary MPSP functions.

For example, a specific group of people may be responsible for performing MPSP. Let's call those people "production planners" and "master schedulers." We can place those people in a particular slot in an organizational structure. However, let's consider who else might be concerned with the processing results of MPSP.

1. Top management wants to review planned production against production targets. They also want to have a long-term view of when existing labor and machining capacities will be exceeded.
2. Operational management would like to know in advance when overtime or an extra shift is required to meet demand.
3. Inventory management wants to see the impact of planned production against anticipated demand on the levels of inventory, period by period.
4. Purchasing would like to be aware of those long lead-time items that are required, to avoid missing potential customer orders in the future.
5. Marketing would like to see how the plant intends to meet the anticipated customer demand. When, and by how much, is demand over or under planned production?

As you can see, MPSP relates to and involves many company personnel. Many of the other functional areas in a manufacturing company do not require the same degree of management attention.

Appendix I illustrates how personnel are structured based on their concerns via an organizational approach. It does not show how MPSP, as a function, relates to other manufacturing functions.

The second approach to understanding functional relationships can be illustrated with a series of charts. Figure 1.1 is an overview chart showing how MPSP fits into a typical manufacturing company.

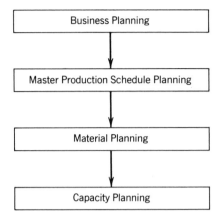

FIGURE 1.1   Overview of where MPSP fits.

The "level of concern" varies widely across these four major planning areas. Business planning is concerned with where we want to drive the business during the next five to ten years. Master production schedule planning deals with planning the production to support the business plan for the next two to three years. Material planning is the process of determining the materials (ordering and receipt) to support the Master Production Schedule for the next six months to a year. And finally, capacity planning deals with *now*. This function is concerned with how to get the product built (with the received material) or, more specifically, how to schedule those work centers that typically cause bottleneck problems.

To expand on the previous chart, Figure 1.2 illustrates how MPSP relates to a basic set of 12 manufacturing functions.

From business planning, MPSP receives production targets and general management guidelines. Forecasting provides statistical forecasts at required planning levels. Customer order servicing provides MPSP with actual sales information.

Another way of defining the MPSP inputs is as follows:

1. Business planning—What we would like to plan to build and sell.
2. Forecasting—Based on sales history and economic indicators, what we probably ought to plan to build and sell.
3. Customer order servicing—What we are actually selling.

Master production schedule planning also has inputs from engineering and production data control and inventory management. The engineering and production data control function provides structure data for bill of material and product family structuring. It also provides work center/facility and routing information for resource planning.

The input from inventory management is inventory status information. The

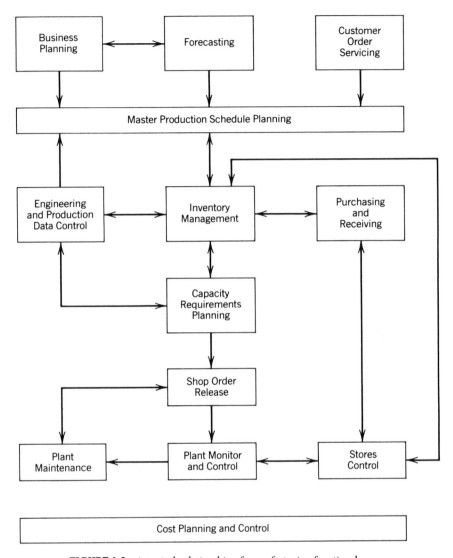

FIGURE 1.2 A typical relationship of manufacturing functional areas.

Material Requirements Planning (MRP), a subfunction of inventory management.

Master production schedule planning as a major functional area is composed of four subfunctions, as shown in Figure 1.3.

Demand analysis planning
Master production planning

Master schedule planning

Resource planning

Demand analysis planning is the process of identifying anticipated customer demand, period by period, across some horizon of time. The logic used within demand analysis may be the same or different as it applies to the two other functions of Master Production Planning (MPP) and Master Schedule Planning (MSP). For example, for one company both MPP and MSP may receive net demand data for the same horizon of time from demand analysis. However, another company may wish demand analysis to provide gross demand only for a three-year horizon to MPP, and net demand data for a one-year horizon to MSP.

Master production planning aggregates the demand for items into groups or families. These families provide a planner with an "ease of use" capability. For example, it is easier to plan production for 40 families (with 20 items per family) than for 800 items. The product families are used for many purposes. They are checked against production targets, against available resources, and against the current production plans being used by MSP.

When new family production plans have been developed and balanced, the resulting item production plans are passed to MSP.

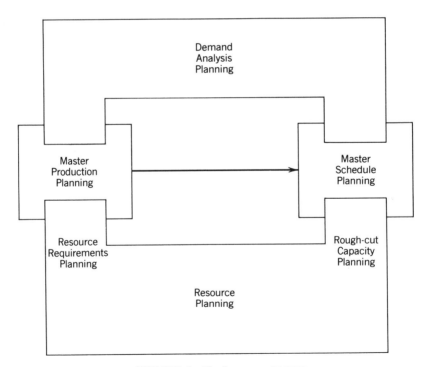

FIGURE 1.3 The functions of MPSP.

Master schedule planning accepts the item production plans from MPP and lot sizes them. A lot size may be for a quantity of one, or for 1000, or for any designated quantity. The lot size is usually based on physical constraints (such as the size of a mixing tank as related to a standard batch quantity) or economic constraints (such as the cost of a machine setup). These lot-sized quantities are called "planned orders." The planned orders are passed to MRP in inventory management.

There are some key distinctions in the planning logic between MPP and MSP. Master production planning deals with families of items with a large period size bucket (such as a month) across a long horizon (such as three years). Master schedule planning deals with individual items instead of families. The item quantities are grouped into planned orders. The period size is usually smaller (such as a week) than that used in MPP. The horizon is also normally shorter (such as one year) than that used in MPP.

Let's consider an example of the distinctions between MPP and MSP. Assume that we have a product family in MPP that has monthly buckets and a one-year horizon. The family is composed of items A and B. The family production plan could have the following quantities per period:

	Month											
	J	F	M	A	M	J	J	A	S	O	N	D
Family	76	96	112	112	104	92	92	92	84	84	84	80

The item production plans that are passed to MSP have the following planned period quantities.

	Month											
	J	F	M	A	M	J	J	A	S	O	N	D
Item A	12	24	32	40	40	40	52	60	72	64	52	40
Item B	64	72	80	72	64	52	40	32	12	20	32	40
Total	76	96	112	112	104	92	92	92	84	84	84	80

For this simplified example, let's make some additional assumptions.

1. The MSP horizon is three months.
2. All months have four weeks (a later chapter discusses period conversion logic of months to weeks).
3. Item A is lot sized into quantities of 10.
4. Item B is lot sized into quantities of 50.

The MSP period quantities are as shown below when the period size conversion is made.

Month	Jan.	Feb.	Mar.
Item A	12	24	32
Item B	64	72	80

Week	1	2	3	4	1	2	3	4	1	2	3	4
Item A	3	3	3	3	6	6	6	6	8	8	8	8
Item B	16	16	16	16	18	18	18	18	20	20	20	20

We have assumed that the lot size for Item A is 10. We planned to produce three in the first week of January, but we cannot—we have to make 10. Therefore if 10 are produced in week one of January, the 10 will consume the planned three of week one, the planned three of week two, the planned three of week three and one of the planned three of week four. Since two of item A in week four are not consumed by the original order, another order must be received at this time. The planned orders necessary to satisfy both item production plans are summarized below.

	Jan.				Feb.				Mar.			
Week	1	2	3	4	1	2	3	4	1	2	3	4
Item A	10			10	10			10	10	10		10
Item B	50			50			50		50			50

The MPP item plan was for a quantity per monthly period for a one-year horizon. The MSP item plan was for planned order quantities per weekly period for a three-month horizon.

The fourth functional area of MPSP shown in Figure 1.3 was resource planning. It interfaces to both MPP and MSP. Although the basic logic for resource planning to support both MPP and MSP is similar, the purposes for the support are different. At the MPP level, we need to know how much labor, machining, or costs are necessary in each planning period for a given family production plan. This process is called "resource requirements planning." The intent is twofold.

1. Find out if the resources required for the period quantities of the Family

Production Plan are actually available in the plant. For example, consider the following situation regarding resources.

| Resources | | | | | | Month | | | | | | | Yearly |
	J	F	M	A	M	J	J	A	S	O	N	D	Total
Required	600	650	700	710	700	650	600	600	600	580	610	620	7620
Available	650	650	650	650	650	650	650	650	600	600	650	650	7700
Net	50	0	(50)	(60)	(50)	0	50	50	0	20	40	30	80

For the year, the example requires 7620 (of let's say machining hours). There are 7700 hours available. At this annual level, we might feel that we are in good shape. However, when viewed in monthly periods, we can see that a problem exists in the periods of March, April, and May. We could make up the March shortage by building ahead in January, where resources are available, but we still would have shortages in April and May.

2. Find out the major trends of required resources. We might see, for example, that direct labor hours will double in two years. We need to plan how and from where the required personnel will be recruited.

As you saw previously, planned order quantities for specific items do not necessarily match the MPP period quantities. The resource testing performed at the MSP level is called "rough-cut capacity planning." It could be done exactly like resource requirements planning was done at the MPP level, but it normally isn't, due to the data volume. At the MPP level, we may have had 40 families (of 20 items per family) that we resource tested. At the MSP level, we have 800 items (20 $\times$ 40 = 800). Instead of doing a test of 800 items against all work centers, most companies will test the items only against critical or bottleneck work centers.

The general concept of capacity planning can be summarized as existing at three different levels in a manufacturing company.

1. MPP resource planning: Resource requirements planning performed at a family level to determine the feasibility of producing the Family Production Plans.

2. MSP resource planning: Rough-cut capacity planning performed at an item level to determine if bottlenecks will occur in critical work centers when planned lot-sized orders are released.

3. Capacity requirements planning (CRP): This is outside the scope of MPSP. It is normally performed after MRP (Material Requirements Planning) processing is accomplished to determine if capacity exists to produce the planned items at a specific workcenter the next shift, the next day, or the next week.

This has been a very general overview of MPSP. The following sections will consider who needs MPSP and give more detail on MPSP functions.

WHO NEEDS MPSP?

There are many opinions on who needs MPSP. Most of the opinions exist however, due to a lack of understanding of the functions within MPSP. Let's consider some of the more classic opinions.

"I don't have a computer, so I don't need MPSP."

This is a real "cart before the horse" example. You do not get a computer and then decide that you will do MPSP. Normally you perform the functions of MPSP manually until the data volumes or response times become unsatisfactory, and then you get a computer to assist you.

Jim: "I don't do MPSP and I don't need to."
Joe: "Do you analyze the source of your potential customer demands?"
Jim: "Sure, Jack does that."
Joe: "Do you group your models, options, or products for long-term resource planning?"
Jim: "Sure, Bill does that."
Joe: "How do you group planned items quantities into orders for material planning?"
Jim: "Fred does that. He's a smart guy. He's got a good feeling about how big a load the shops can handle."

MPSP is obviously being performed in the above scenario. It is being done manually, and there is nothing wrong with that if the company needs are being met. If, however, inventory is out of control, MRP is nervous, and ship dates are frequently missed, then a data processing approach might be an improvement over a pure manual approach.

"I don't need MPSP because I'm a custom job shop."

This may well be a valid answer. If a second product is never started before the first product is completed, then the planning is simple. Or is it? What is the product? Is it a widget or an aircraft carrier? The implied assumption is that since I do not need all four MPSP functions, then I do not need MPSP. A company that builds aircraft carriers one at a time may not need demand analysis or MPP, but they could probably use MSP and resource planning to balance the workload in the shops.

"MPSP develops planned orders and I don't use orders. I build according to a weekly rate schedule. I'm a flow shop."

First let's consider the differences between a flow shop and a job shop. There are two ways to control production, either by planned order quantities (a job shop) or by a periodic build rate schedule (a flow shop). However, this simple categorization is too broad. Each of these two groups can be further subdivided according to the unit of measure (U/M) that is used. If the U/M is in terms of each item or multiples of each item, then it is discrete. If the U/M is in terms of gallons, square feet, or some similar volume measure, then it is continuous.

These groupings may be categorized as follows:

Job shop (controlled by orders)
  Discrete job shop (U/M equals "each")
    Typical Product: Specialized machine tool, to specification air conditioner, customized airplane
  Continuous job shop (U/M equals "volume")
    Typical product: Specialty chemicals
Flow shop (controlled by schedules)
  Discrete flow shop (U/M equals "each")
    Typical product: TV sets, automobiles, residential air conditioners, toys, batteries
  Continuous flow shop (U/M equals "volume")
    Typical product: Oil

From this grouping analysis, it can be seen that MPSP primarily applies to the discrete areas, for both job shops and flow shops. If a rate schedule, instead of planned orders, is required to run the plant, then the period quantities from MPP could be used directly, and possibly MSP could even be ignored.

Not every company needs everything that is potentially available from MPSP. However, due to a lack of understanding of the functions within MPSP, many companies feel that they do not need MPSP. Every manufacturer that is a discrete job shop or a discrete flow shop needs MPSP either partially or in total. The need has nothing to do with how the function is performed (as via computer), only that the function is performed.

The next chapter presents a more detailed overview on each of the MPSP functional areas.

CHAPTER TWO

AN OVERVIEW OF MPSP FUNCTIONS

DEMAND ANALYSIS PLANNING

The previous chapter should have given you a general understanding of what MPSP is and how it relates to other functional areas. Figure 2.1 is a summary of how the functions within MPSP relate to external functions. Let us now review each of the four MPSP functions in a little more depth.

Demand analysis is illustrated in Figure 2.2. There are four fundamental sets of input data necessary for demand analysis.

1. Management projections—This data is normally used either as a guideline or when management wishes to disregard or override the statistical projections.
2. Statistical projections—This is the data that result from the processing of a forecasting function. Pure statistical projections may be adjusted by management projections and external economic indicators.
3. Actual sales—These are booked orders, either to actual customers or to internal facilities, such as to another warehouse or distribution location. Actual sales can be orders scheduled to ship in this period or in some future period.
4. Available inventory—This is the inventory balance on hand (BOH) minus any safety stock and hedged or build-ahead inventory. Allocations of inventory to existing sales orders are not used in the calculation of available inventory because they have already been considered in the demand calculation.

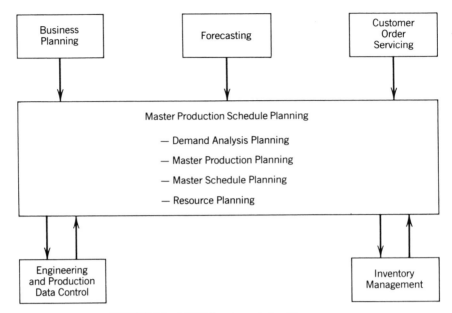

FIGURE 2.1 MPSP function relationship summary.

The first step in demand analysis is the identification of those items to be planned. This decision process will vary widely from one company to the next. For example, a company might sell 10,000 unique end items. The major material content of these end items is located in 40 major assemblies. The major assemblies are produced from 40,000 components and raw materials. The logical MPSP planning level for this company is the major assembly level, since the volume allows for ease of management.

Another company might produce 250 different end items. There might be very few common parts or assemblies between the end items. This company would probably plan at the end item level.

Frequently a company initiates an item-coding structure to designate how an individual item is to be planned. Such a structure could be based on the following considerations:

Item is to be production planned only.

Item is to be master scheduled only.

Item is to be both production planned and master scheduled.

Item is to be planned by MRP.

The next step in demand analysis is to identify the data source(s) which is to be used for each coded item. Item A may be a stable make-to-stock service part. For Item A, the statistical projections may be used as the data source. Item B may be a new product that is planned to be in production in nine

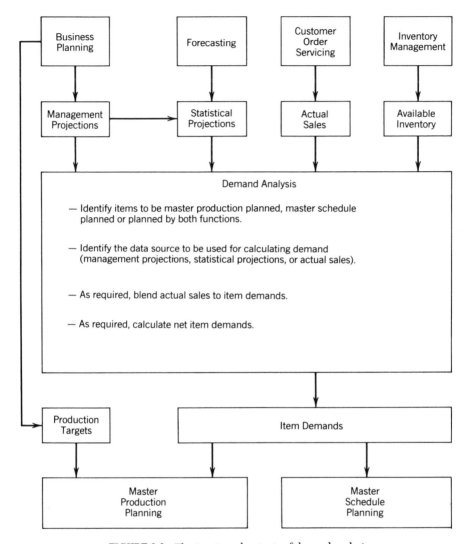

FIGURE 2.2   The inputs and outputs of demand analysis.

months. There are no statistical projections (no sales history to build the projections) or actual sales data. Management projections may be used for Item B. Item C is a heavily engineered, custom-designed item. No manufacturing is started on Item C until an actual customer order is booked. Probably, only actual sales would be used for Item C. Item D does have historical sales data from which statistical projections can be made. However, this forecasted information is considered to have some potential error, possibly because the historical sales data were accumulated during an economic recession. To increase the accuracy of the data, Item D could have statistical projection data blended with actual sales data. The use of available inventory could apply to all of the item examples if net demand was a desired output.

It is necessary that the data sources (format, period sizes, item levels, etc.) are an exact match to the items to be scheduled by MPSP or a data translation program is required. Often, however, when MPSP is initially installed, this is not the case. Consider this example. Marketing provides period-by-period forecast data (statistical projections) for Model 842. A Model 842 is composed of a standard parts group, two variants, and two options. One of the two variants must be selected by a customer to make a valid product, but an option may or may not be selected by the customer. The repair centers for this company send in a forecast (statistical projections) for service part demands. One of the options in a Model 842 is sold as a service part. Also, a component in the standard parts group is sold as a service part.

Figure 2.3 illustrates a product structure of the above example. Forecasts are received for Model 842s from Marketing, and for option 2's and bushings from repair center management. The items to be managed by MPSP are:

Option 1 (selected 40% of the time)
Option 2 (selected 25% of the time)

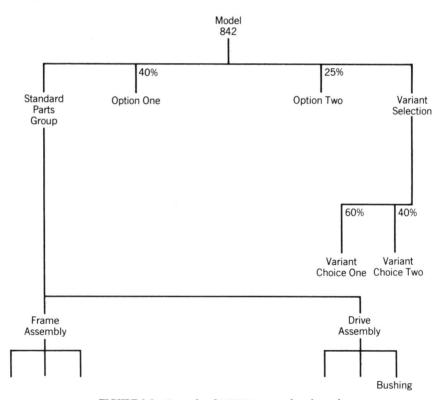

FIGURE 2.3 Example of MPSP items to be planned.

Variant 1 (selected 60% of the time)
Variant 2 (selected 40% of the time)
Bushings

By now you should be starting to understand the problem. There are three potential ways to address the problem of how to identify the right quantities at the right level for each MPSP item.

For the first approach, do not accept a forecast for model 842s from Marketing. Require Marketing to provide forecast quantities for each of the possible individual Model 842 configurations. These are the possible mixes for this example.

Model	Variant 1	Variant 2	Option 1	Option 2
842-1	X			
842-2	X		X	
842-3	X			X
842-4		X		
842-5		X	X	
842-6		X		X

Note that now you are requesting Marketing to provide you with six forecasts instead of one. This is a very simple example. Often there are hundreds of configuration combinations. If you elect this technique to address the problem, be aware of the impact that your request will have on Marketing.

A second approach is to accept the model forecast and then explode the planning structure to the correct MPSP item planning level. Next add forecasts together for all similar items. For example, assume the forecasts are as follows:

Item	Period 1	2	3	4	5	6	7	8	9	10	11	12
Model 842	420	410	400	400	400	410	420	430	440	450	440	430
Option 2	14	16	18	20	22	20	16	12	8	4	0	8
Bushing	200	200	200	220	260	300	400	300	250	220	190	200

The first step is to identify the required quantity of MPSP items from the Model 842 forecast. Exploding the Model 842 forecast by the mix percentages yields the following quantities per period.

	Period											
	1	2	3	4	5	6	7	8	9	10	11	12
Model 842	420	410	400	400	400	410	420	430	440	450	440	430
Option 1	168	164	160	160	160	164	168	172	176	180	176	172
Option 2	105	103	100	100	100	103	105	108	110	113	110	108
Variant 1	252	246	240	240	240	246	252	258	264	270	264	258
Variant 2	168	164	160	160	160	164	168	172	176	180	176	172
Bushing	420	410	400	400	400	410	420	430	440	450	440	430

The repair and exploded model forecast data may now be added together for those items sold as service parts.

	Period											
	1	2	3	4	5	6	7	8	9	10	11	12
Option 2												
Model Requirements	105	103	100	100	100	103	105	108	110	113	110	108
Repair Requirements	14	16	18	20	22	20	16	12	8	4	0	8
Total	119	119	118	120	122	123	121	120	118	117	110	116
Bushing												
Model Requirements	420	410	400	400	400	410	420	430	440	450	440	430
Repair Requirements	200	200	200	200	260	300	400	300	250	220	190	200
Total	620	610	600	620	660	710	820	730	690	670	630	630

The MPSP items may then be summarized as shown below.

	Period											
	1	2	3	4	5	6	7	8	9	10	11	12
Option 1	168	164	160	160	160	164	168	172	176	180	176	172
Option 2	119	119	118	120	122	123	121	120	118	117	110	116
Variant 1	252	246	240	240	240	246	252	258	264	270	264	258
Variant 2	168	164	160	160	160	164	168	172	176	180	176	172
Bushing	620	610	600	620	660	710	820	730	690	670	630	630

Note that the above example has lumped end-item and repair-service part forecasts together. Sometimes these are managed separately by different systems.

The third approach is probably the simplest, but normally is used only if a computer is available for processing.

Consider that the company probably does not just produce Model 842s. They also make 845s, 960s, and 980s. All of these models have configuration problems similar to those of the 842s. You have already decided that to do MPP, you are going to group the options, variants, and service parts into product families based on the consumption of common resources. As a result, you have defined four product families. You request a forecast for the marketing of each of the four families.

Your request has the following impact on Marketing. The model forecasts must be exploded to the proper planning level. Multiple projections for the same item(s) must be added together. The individual item projections must then be aggregated to a family level and supplied to you for input to MPP.

Of the three approaches, there really is no universal best approach that applies to everyone. Each company must utilize the technique that is effective in their individual environment.

Note that if model data, for example, has been exploded to some lower planning level, then actual sales data must also be exploded to the same level so that the blending action can take place (if applicable) for a particular item. The actual blending process is discussed in a later chapter.

Finally, net demands are calculated (again, if applicable). This is a simple arithmetic calculation to subtract available inventory from the gross demand, as shown in the following example for bushings for which a quantity of 1930 was originally available.

	Period											
	1	2	3	4	5	6	7	8	9	10	11	12
Gross	620	610	600	620	660	710	820	730	690	670	630	630
Available	1930	1310	700	100	0	0	0	0	0	0	0	0
Net	0	0	0	520	660	710	820	730	690	670	630	630

The resulting item demands (frequently both the net and the gross demand data) are supplied by demand analysis to MPP and MSP, as required for planning.

MASTER PRODUCTION PLANNING

Master production planning is illustrated in Figure 2.4. There are four basic sets of input data to MPP.

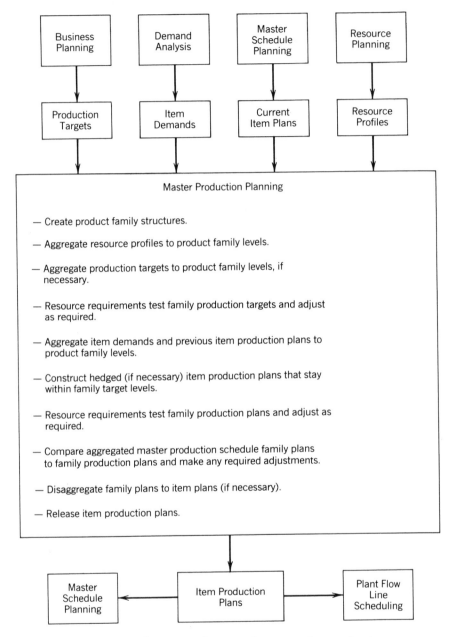

FIGURE 2.4 The inputs and outputs of master production planning.

1. Production targets—These are established by management as the acceptable or desired production levels of each family of MPSP items that are to be production planned. These are established at a family and not an item level.

The production targets may vary by time, and they may also be supplied at limit settings. Management may decide that 500 a day is a desired target for the 2nd quarter (for a product family), but 700 a day is the desired target for the balance of the year.

A desired rate is only one of three possible targets that management may provide. The three can be defined as:

Production minimum, which implies that the production line will shut down if the actual rate falls below this amount.

Production desired, which is normally the most cost-effective rate at which to produce the product.

Production maximum, which is the most that can be produced per day within the available capacity constraints.

Notice that we have discussed production targets in terms of daily rates as opposed to weekly or monthly rates. This is because there is a variable number of workdays within a week or month due to holidays and plant vacation shut-downs.

2.   Item demands—These are the MPSP item demands that were developed in demand analysis.

3.   Current item plans—The last time that MPP was performed, item production plans were released to MSP. These were converted to planned orders and scheduled. Now a new MPP plan is being constructed and the current item plans are used for comparison purposes.

4.   Resource profiles—This is a set of data that defines the plant resources necessary to produce a quantity of one MPSP item. The data includes offsets. For example, if it takes four periods to produce an "A", and an "A" is planned to ship in period six, then the resource profile for "A" shows the plant resources required in periods six, five, four, and three.

The first step of MPP is the creation of product families. This function involves major considerations, and a full chapter is devoted to it later in the book. A product family is a group of MPSP items. The grouping or product family structuring is a large initial effort when MPSP is first being implemented. After the initial effort, it is only a matter of identifying into which product families new items will be included.

Once product family structures are known, the resource profiles may be aggregated to the product family level (if standard item to family mix percentages are used). Resource profiles are initially provided at an item and not a family level.

If the production targets had also been provided at the item level (as opposed to a family level, which is preferable), then these quantities would also have to be aggregated to a family level.

Now, if either the resource profiles had changed (for example, two old milling machines were replaced with a single new one) or the production targets had changed, then testing the family targets against the family resource profiles should be performed. It is simple for management to say that for each of these 20 families, here are the production targets. However, if testing those targets against the profiles of available resources indicates that 2000 extra people have to be hired in period five and then layed off in period eight, it might be advisable to show management the potential resource problem and allow them to adjust their targets or commit to a new labor program.

Once the family production targets are considered to be valid, the item demands from demand analysis can be aggregated to the family level. These family demands can then be tested against family targets. It is often the case that although the horizon totals (for instance, across three years) indicate that demand can be satisfied with production targets, period "X" has a demand spike that cannot be satisfied by that period's production. A process is then applied that is called hedging, or building ahead. Consider the following situation:

	Period					
	1	2	3	4	5	6
Family production target	300	300	300	300	300	300
Family demand	200	250	300	350	325	300

The demand in periods four and five exceeds the production target. Hedging is done by building ahead to meet demand in the future. (Note that this implies increasing inventory levels. Another option is to lose sales in periods four and five.) Hedges are constructed as shown by the following example:

	Period					
	1	2	3	4	5	6
Family production target	300	300	300	300	300	300
Family demand	200	250	300	350	325	300
Starting family production plan	200	250	300	350	325	300
1st hedge		+25			−25	
Resulting production plan	200	275	300	350	300	300
2nd hedge		+25		−25		
Resulting production plan	200	300	300	325	300	300
3rd hedge	+25			−25		
Final family production plan	225	300	300	300	300	300
Total Hedges	+25	+50		−50	−25	

We now have a production plan that meets demand and stays within the production targets. A key consideration in hedging is the process for managing the build ahead or hedge inventory. The inventory created by build aheads (hedging) has to be reserved for when demand is planned to occur.

At this point, a potentially new production plan exists for release to MSP. However, prior to release, it is a normal desire to compare this "new plan" to the plan that is already being used (the "old plan") by MSP. The purpose for the comparison is to reduce nervousness (constant change) of the system. For example, the old plan was to make 245 in period four. The new plan is to make 243 in period four. Depending on the material and manufacturing lead times, the decision might well be able to make the original 245 or take an average and plan for 244.

When all adjustments have been completed, the item production plans can be released. Disaggregation may or may not be required, depending on how the product families were created.

Item production plans can be used directly to schedule a plant flow line or to feed MSP.

MASTER SCHEDULE PLANNING

The inputs to MSP, consisting of item demands, item production plans, resource profiles, and inventory status are illustrated in Figure 2.5. Each of these has already been discussed in previous sections.

The main purpose of MSP is to convert a general item production plan (such as 200 of Item A in month six) to specific realistic orders (such as four orders of 50 each for Item A in weeks one, two, three, and four, of month six) for input to MRP.

The first step in the MSP process is to convert planning bucket sizes. For example, the buckets used in MPP may have been months. Those used in MSP may be weeks. The quantities per month have to be converted to quantities per week.

Then, based on some lot-sizing criteria, the quantities are grouped (lumped) into orders. These orders may be lot sized into a quantity of one, a quantity of 5000, or any amount. In MPP, quantities of planned items were resource tested by a process known as "resource requirements planning." These quantities were made available to MSP. Now two things have changed, the quantity per period and the period (bucket) size. For example, MPP may have produced the following item production plan for Item A.

Monthly Quantities

1	2	3	4	5	6	7	8	9	10	11	12
20	20	20	20	24	24	24	24	28	28	32	32

Within MPP, Item A passed resource testing. Now the quantities are passed to MSP. The lot-size criteria for Item A states that the minimum order is for a quantity of 50. If we can assume, for this example, that there are four weeks to a month, the MSP planned orders would be as follows:

Month	1				2				3			
Monthly quantity	20				20				20			
Week	1	2	3	4	1	2	3	4	1	2	3	4
Order quantity	50										50	

Month	4				5				6			
Monthly quantity	20				24				24			
Week	1	2	3	4	1	2	3	4	1	2	3	4
Order quantity								50				

Month	7				8				9			
Monthly quantity	24				24				28			
Week	1	2	3	4	1	2	3	4	1	2	3	4
Order quantity				50								50

Month	10				11				12			
Monthly quantity	28				32				32			
Week	1	2	3	4	1	2	3	4	1	2	3	4
Order quantity					50							

In MPP we planned for production of 20 in January, 20 in February, 20 in March, and 20 in April. Now we are planning orders for 50 in January, none in February, 50 in March, and none in April. Resource testing must again be performed, but for a different reason. We now need to know if these lot-sized orders will cause bottlenecks in the critical work centers. This process is called "rough-cut capacity planning."

If the planned orders pass resource testing, there are several reviews that are normally made to insure that this plan is realistic. The planned production is compared to the anticipated demand to determine if any sales are going to be missed. In addition, an inventory projection is made. This projection says, "If I plan to produce this amount, and I anticipate that I will sell this amount, and the available quantity I have right now is this amount; what will be the impact on my inventory, period by period, across the horizon?" Techniques to display these sets of data are discussed in later chapters.

A very valuable output of MPS is available-to-promise (ATP) data. This is normally supplied to the personnel who are booking new orders from customers. Consider that you are an order entry clerk. The customer wants to know when his or her order will be ready. You could say tomorrow (as many people do-

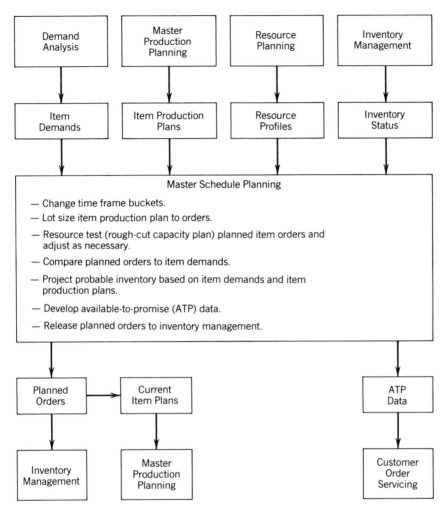

FIGURE 2.5   The inputs and outputs of master schedule planning.

—unfortunately), or next year, or that you don't know. Or, you could look at data like the following.

	Period					
	1	2	3	4	5	6
Planned production receipts	20		20		20	
Previous booked orders	15	4	5	6	0	0
Available to promise	1	1	9	9	20	20

A new order quantity of one may be booked into periods one or two. As soon as a new order is booked into either of these periods, the ATP quantity for periods one and two goes to zero.

Finally, MSP releases its planned orders to MRP (a subfunction of inventory management).

There are a variety of item details that have not been covered in this overview; these items are covered in following sections.

RESOURCE PLANNING

As you can tell by Figure 2.6, resource planning contains some data sources that have not been previously discussed. Note that different software application systems will tend to structure (format) this data in different ways, depending on the intent of the software when it was written. The key input considerations however, are listed below.

1. Work center costs—A work center may be one machine (or person) or a group of machines (or persons). Associated with each work center are certain rates that are applied to the number of hours an item consumes while it is in the work center. Some of these costs are overhead costs, set-up costs (of machine or assembly line), and run costs per piece.

2. Routings—These are the descriptions of what work is to be done to what piece, in the correct work sequence. A routing is normally organized into a sequence of operations, or work steps. Each operation may take place in a different work center. The starts and finishes of a routing are usually stocking points. A routing starts when one or more parts are pulled from stock. Operations are performed, and the resulting part or assembly is put back into stock, which completes the routing. Every operation step for each item identifies some basic information, such as time in input queue, set-up time, run time, time in output queue, and move time to the next operation.

3. Structure data—This is normal bill-of-material (BOM) structure data. It says that Item X is made out of an "A" and a "B." The "A" is purchased. The "B" is made out of a "1" and a "2." In addition to manufactured, purchased, and structure data, it also provides lead times (to manufacture or to purchase) and quantities required for the next higher level of assembly.

Resource planning supports both MPP and MSP. The items to be processed by resource planning have to be identified as to whether they will be planned by MPP, MSP, or both.

The purpose of this function is to identify, if we make "one" of this item, how much of what resources will be required and when. This is a process that

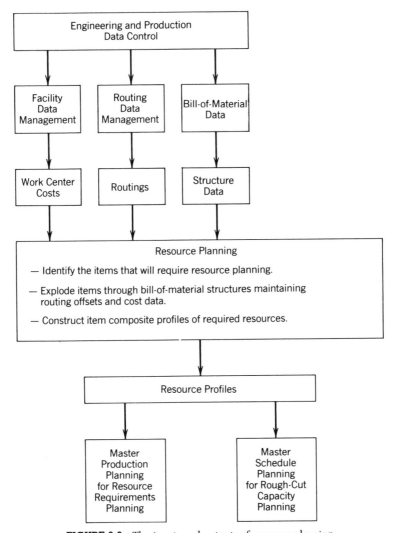

FIGURE 2.6 The inputs and outputs of resource planning.

involves exploding the structure data, relating it to the routings, and extending it by work center cost data. For example, it takes one week to assemble an "X" out of an "A" and a "B." The assembly process takes five days, using five operations (one operation per day). An "X" could be required on day seven. Operation five consumes day seven. Operation four consumes day six, and so forth. At the conclusion of this single-level explosion, we know which work center is involved and when. ("When" means offset time from the planned finish date.) This can then be extended (hours times costs per hour) to develop a composite profile for an item. The composite is a summary of all of the explosions at all levels of the structure data. The actual composite is not for a specific date (as day seven in the above example), but rather a general profile that can be applied to any date.

The item resource profile defines what resources are required when, to produce an item. These profiles are supplied to both MPP and MSP, although the two functions have a slightly different use for the data.

Next, we will review some of the methods that are often utilized to create some of the data used to drive an MPSP system.

PART TWO

BUSINESS PLANNING AND FORECAST DATA MANAGEMENT CONSIDERATIONS

CHAPTER THREE

A MAKE-TO-STOCK
AND PACKAGE-TO-ORDER
COMPANY

THE FAMILY CONCEPT

Many companies utilize both sales families and product families. Before we proceed with how companies use these families, we should understand the purpose of each.

A sales family is a structure technique employed by Marketing to do forecasting. It consists of taking all of the products (end items, models, etc.) that have similar sales trends throughout the year and grouping them into a single family. Consider a company that manufactures the following products.

Lawn mowers—Home use; four models (LM1, LM2, LM3, and LM4)
Lawn mowers—Commercial use; two models (LMC1 and LMC2)
Chain saws—Home use; three models (CH1, CH2, and CH3)
Chain saws—Commercial use; one model (CHC1)
Snow blowers—Home use; two models (SB1 and SB2)

The company makes the following assumptions. Lawn mowers have a seasonal peak in April. Snow blowers have a seasonal peak in December. Home-use chain saws also have a seasonal peak in December, when the average home-owner decides that it's time to cut some wood for the fireplace. The commercial chain saw user cuts firewood all summer long so that he or she has some to sell when winter arrives. Commercial chain saws therefore have a seasonal peak in April.

Figure 3.1 illustrates how this company might structure their sales families. Note that the type of product may not have anything to do with the family into which the product is designated.

The advantage of using a sales family (SF) is that it simplifies the forecasting process. In the above example, only two forecasts need to be made, one for SF 1 and one for SF 2. If families had not been used, then each model of each product would have been forecasted, and 12 forecasts instead of two would have been created.

Mix percentages of items within the SF also need to be known. For each product within a family (such as LM1 in SF 1), we need to know the percentage of LM1s that make up SF 1. For example, if LM1s constitute 15% of SF 1, and the forecast indicates a quantity of 120 SF 1s are required for a particular period, we can then calculate that 18 LM1s are required (120 times 15% equals 18).

The second type of family is called a "product family." Sometimes it is also referred to as a "production family" or a "product group." This is a structure technique used in MPP, and the structuring logic varies based on the needs of individual companies.

A product family (PF) may be structured:

Exactly the same as a sales family (based on sales trends)

Based on cost groups (high-cost items in PF 1, medium cost items in PF 2, etc.)

Based on a grouping of the consumption of similar machine and/or labor hours

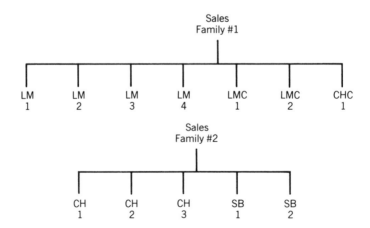

FIGURE 3.1   An example of sales family structures.

Based on a distinction between standard and customized products

Based on some unique material or component requirements

The classical definition of how to structure a product family is "All items that consume approximately the same quantity of the same type of resources should be structured in the same product family." The problem with the classical definition is that:

A "resource" can be anything: cost, number of salesmen, labor hours, floor space, and so on.

Companies tend to structure product families based on what they feel is practical for their own needs (which could create a family for standard products, one for products offered with options, and one for pure customized products).

Now that the two basic types of families are understood, we will review approaches that companies might take in the definition of the data that is utilized by MPSP. Two different companies are reviewed: a make-to-stock (MTS) and package-to-order company, and a make-to-order (MTO) Company.

The MTS company has three basic groups of products. These are private labeled and sold to three different customers. Each of the three product groups has variations related to packaging, private label data, and overpack considerations. The MTO company markets four basic products, but it seldom sells the specific machines pictured in their catalog. There are customer-allowed choices on bucket size, engine type, hydraulics, emission control, and so forth.

The MTS company is a combination of various flow lines that attempt to build to forecast (hopefully not to stock with private labels) and still meet actual customer demand on the desired ship dates. Their goal is to plan properly, so that they do not upset the plant by reacting.

The MTO company builds buckets to stock in anticipation of need for a specific model/option configuration. Mostly, this company is a job shop. They do not build an end item until they have a customer order. Their goal is to perform some general planning based on forecasts, but then to react to customer demand as rapidly as possible by processing the customer order without incurring bottlenecks in the shop.

THE ENVIRONMENT OF THE MAKE-TO-STOCK COMPANY

The MTS Company manufactures toy cars and trucks. The old standby has been product group 602X, which is a toy car consisting of an upper casting, a lower casting, a plastic windshield, two axles, and four wheels. It is sold in one of three different carrying cases. Each case holds a different number of cars. A private label is attached to the carrying case. Three different overpack techniques are used, depending on which size of carrying case is used. The result is a "carton of toy cars," which is the end item that is actually shipped to the customer.

Figure 3.2 is a pictorial illustration of product group 602X as viewed by Manufacturing. Although it shows a realistic representation of how the product is assembled, it is difficult to use for planning purposes as it is structured. The

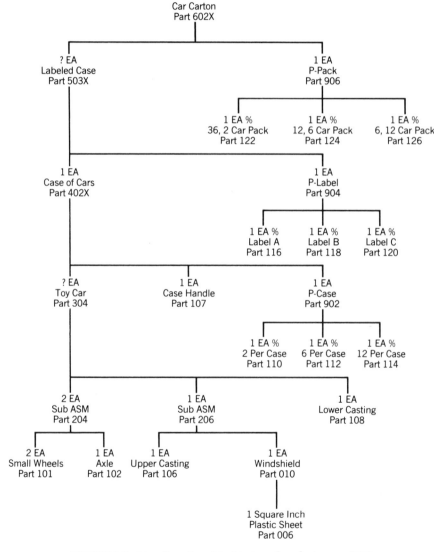

FIGURE 3.2 Manufacturing pictorial view of product group 602X.

number of cars (Part 304) required to make one case of cars (Part 402) depends upon which case (Part 110, 112, or 114) was selected.

Also, even if the percentages were shown for the variants, the situation is not that clear. Not all customers purchase all combinations of cars in each case, as shown below.

	Customers		
Product Group 602X	A	B	C
2-Car case	X		X
6-Car case	X	X	X
12-Car case	X	X	

The second product group of The MTS Company is 502X. This a toy dump truck. It consists of a body casting, a bed casting, a pivot pin, a plastic windshield, two axles, and four wheels.

This product group has some slight deviations form 602X. No customers wish to purchase the trucks packaged 12 per carrying case. All customers want to buy the trucks packaged individually in a box (no carrying case).

Figure 3.3 is a pictorial illustration of product group 502X as viewed by Manufacturing. As can be seen, similar problems exist in using this structure for planning purposes, although it does represent how the product is assembled. The number of toy trucks (Part 450) to make a box or case of trucks (Part 550) is unknown since it depends on the selected case (Part 142, 110, or 112). Also note that the case handle (Part 107) is now an option. Its usage depends on whether a case was selected, as opposed to a box.

As in the previous group, not all customers want all possible combinations, as shown below.

	Customers		
Product Group 502X	A	B	C
1 Truck per box	X	X	X
2-Truck case	X	X	
6-Truck case	X		

The third product group of The MTS Company is 840X. This is an electric car with an injection-molded plastic frame. It has not met with too much success in sales. It consists of a molded body, an electric motor, two rear axles (inserted on each side of the motor), two large rear wheels, a front axle, and two small front wheels.

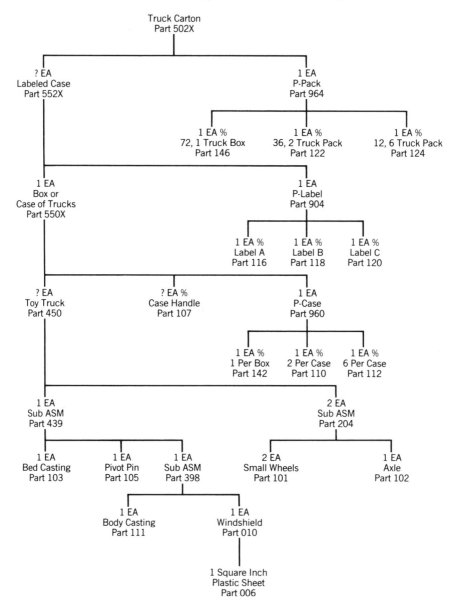

FIGURE 3.3   Manufacturing pictorial view of product group 502X.

Only customers A and C buy this product, and it is only purchased in a two-car carrying case, which decreases some of the possible options.

Figure 3.4 is a pictorial illustration of product group 840X as viewed by Manufacturing. The product structure could be used for planning purposes as it exists.

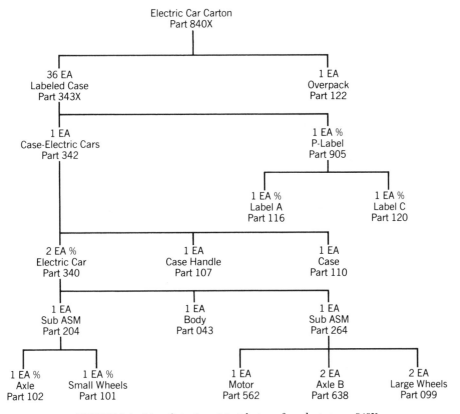

FIGURE 3.4 Manufacturing pictorial view of product group 840X.

The distribution of customer purchases is as follows:

	Customers		
Product Group 502X	A	B	C
2-Electric-car case	X		X

In the following pages, we will consider how The MTS Company might evaluate the previous year's sales activity, make projections, and apply those projections to forecast models.

AN ANALYSIS OF THE PREVIOUS YEAR'S SALES ACTIVITY

An overview analysis that The MTS Company might perform is a simple review of how many dollars of each product group each customer (A, B, and C) is buying, as shown below.

Overview Sales Analysis
(All dollars in thousands)

Product Group	Product Group Sales	Previous Year's Customer Sales		
		A	B	C
602X	$ 32,000	$12,000	$ 16,000	$ 4,000
502X	184,000	78,000	100,000	6,000
840X	5,000	3,000	0	2,000
Totals	$221,000	$93,000	$116,000	$12,000

A second consideration for The MTS Company's review is a mix analysis. What does each product group contribute (by percentage) to total sales? What percentage of sales does each customer contribute to each product group? An example is shown below.

Mix Analysis By Customer and Product Group

Product Group	Group Percentage of Total Sales	Customer	Customer Percentage of Group Sales
602X	14	A	38
		B	50
		C	12
502X	79	A	42
		B	54
		C	4
840X	7	A	60
		B	0
		C	40

Conversely, The MTS Company would probably want to know which customers were the major buyers and which product groups the customers were buying.

Mix Analysis By Product Group and Customer

Customer	Customer Percentage of Total Sales	Product Group	Customer Percentage of Product Group Sales
A	42	602X	13
		502X	84
		840X	3

Mix Analysis By Product Group and Customer (continued)

Customer	Customer Percentage of Total Sales	Product Group	Customer Percentage of Product Group Sales
B	52	602X	14
		502X	86
		840X	0
C	6	602X	33
		502X	50
		840X	17

Due to the option and variant combinations, any specific product group can be broken down to individual end items. The end items can be identified as shown below.

End Items Within Product Groups

Product Group	Item Type	Number Per Box or Case	Customer	End Item Number
602X	Car	2	A	602A
			B	602B
		6	A	602C
			B	602D
			C	602E
		12	A	602F
			B	602G
502X	Truck	1	A	502A
			B	502B
			C	502C
		2	A	502D
			B	502E
		6	A	502F
840X	Electric car	2	A	840A
			C	840B

As part of The MTS Company's analysis of the previous year's sales activity, they also might wish to see the customer distribution of sales by end item within product group, as illustrated below.

Distribution Percent By Customer

Product Group	End Item Number	Customer Percentage of Group Sales		
		A	B	C
602X	602A	50		
	602B			70
	602C	30		
	602D		60	
	602E			30
	602F	20		
	602G		40	
502X	502A	10		
	502B		15	
	502C			100
	502D	60		
	502E		85	
	502F	30		
840X	840A	100		
	840B			100

The previous information represents the summary type analysis that might be done by The MTS Company on the sales data for the previous year.

ESTIMATING THE SALES FOR THE FUTURE YEAR'S ACTIVITY

The MTS Company has identified the following extrinsic variables that might be applied to the future year's projections.

1. The sales for product group 602X (cars) are expected to increase by 28% for all customers.
2. Customer C has declared that they will promote product group 502X (trucks) and triple the previous year's sales.
3. The sales for product group 502X with customers A and B are expected to increase by 20%.
4. Product group 804X (electric cars) sales are expected to decrease by 40%.

The MTS Company applies these projections as follows:

Extrinsic Variables Change Impact
(All dollars in thousands.)

Product Group	Customer	Previous Year Totals	Projected Change	Current Year Projected Sales
602X		$ 32,000		
	A	12,000	Plus 28%	$ 15,360
	B	16,000	Plus 28%	20,480
	C	4,000	Plus 28%	5,120
			Total	$40,960
502X		$184,000		
	A	78,000	Plus 20%	$ 93,600
	B	100,000	Plus 20%	120,000
	C	6,000	Plus 200%	18,000
			Total	$231,600
840X		$ 5,000		
	A	3,000	Minus 40%	$ 1,800
	B	0		
	C	2,000	Minus 40%	1,200
			Total	$ 3,000

Given the previous information, the MTS Company may now wish to perform an analysis of which customers are predicted to buy how much of what product group.

Projected Sales Analysis Overview
(All dollars in thousands.)

Product Group	Product Group Sales	Projected Year Customer Sales		
		A	B	C
602X	$ 40,960	$ 15,360	$ 20,480	$ 5,120
502X	231,600	93,600	120,000	18,000
840X	3,000	1,800	0	1,200
Totals	$275,560	$110,760	$140,480	$24,320

The MTS Company probably feels comfortable with this analysis, but they also would probably like to know where the change will take place and how large it will be. Several analyses can be performed to provide this information as shown below.

Analysis Type By Total Sales
(All dollars in thousands.)

	Previous Year's Amount	Projected Future Year's Amount	Percentage of Change
Total Sales	$221,000	$275,560	Plus 25

By Product Group

Group 602X	$ 32,000	$ 40,960	Plus 28
Group 502X	184,000	231,600	Plus 26
Group 840X	5,000	3,000	Minus 40
Total		$275,560	

By Customer

A	$ 93,000	$110,760	Plus 19
B	116,000	140,480	Plus 21
C	12,000	24,320	Plus 102
Total		$275,560	

By Product Within Customer

Customer	Product Group	Previous Year's Amount	Projected Future Year's Amount	Percentage Change
A	602X	$ 12,000	$ 15,360	Plus 28
	502X	78,000	93,600	Plus 20
	840X	3,000	1,800	Minus 40
B	602X	$ 16,000	$ 20,480	Plus 28
	502X	100,000	120,000	Plus 20
	840X	0	0	0
C	602X	4,000	$ 5,120	Plus 28
	502X	6,000	18,000	Plus 200
	840X	2,000	1,200	Minus 40
	Total		$275,560	

Earlier, The MTS Company did a mix analysis on the previous year's sales activity. They will probably want to perform the same type of analysis with the projected data for the future year. This distribution analysis is illustrated below.

Mix Analysis by Customer and Product Group
(dollars in thousands)

Product Group	Projected Sales	Percentage of Total Sales	Customer	Projected Sales	Percentage of Group Sales
602X	$40,960	15	A	$15,360	38
			B	20,480	50
			C	5,120	12
502X	231,600	84	A	93,600	40
			B	120,000	52
			C	18,000	8
840X	3,000	1	A	1,800	60
			B	0	0
			C	1,200	40
Totals	$275,560			$275,560	

The MTS Company now has some understanding as to their company direction, in terms of dollars.

CONVERSION OF SALES DOLLARS TO UNIT QUANTITIES

The previous section developed useful information for sales, but we need to convert dollar sales predictions to item quantities that can be used with a forecasting model. Since each of the individual end items (602A, 602B, etc.) have different prices, the conversion requires reducing the product groups to the individual items within each product group.

Previously, in the section titled, "An Analysis of the Previous Year's Sales Activity," a customer mix percentage of end items to product groups was illustrated. For purposes of simplicity, let us assume that these mix percentages have not changed for the projected future year. The following are the calculations necessary to derive the end item projected sales dollars.

End Item Projected Sales
(dollars in thousands)

Product Group	Customer Name	Group Projected Sales	End Item	Customer Group Mix Percentage	End Item Projected Sales
602X	A	$15,360	602A	50	$ 7,680
			602C	30	4,608
			602F	20	3,072
	B	20,480	602D	60	12,288
			602G	40	8,192
	C	5,120	602B	70	3,584
			602E	30	1,536
				Total	$40,960
502X	A	$93,600	502A	10	$ 9,360
			502D	60	56,160
			502F	30	28,080
	B	120,000	502B	15	18,000
			502E	85	102,000
	C	18,000	502C	100	18,000
				Total	$231,600
840X	A	$1,800	840A	100	$ 1,800
	C	1,200	840B	100	1,200
				Total	$ 3,000
				Gross Total	$275,560

The end items may now be catagorized by price group. For example, cars packed two per case and 36 cases per carton cost more (and are priced higher) than cars packed 12 per case and six cases per carton. This grouping process is shown below.

Price Groups
(dollars in thousands)

Product Group	Number Per Case	End Items	End Item Projected Sales	Price Group Projected Sales	Price Group	End Item Price Group Mix Percentage
602X	2	602A	$7,680			68
		602B	3,584	$11,264	A	32

Price Groups (continued)
(dollars in thousands)

Product Group	Number Per Case	End Items	End Item Projected Sales	Price Group Projected Sales	Price Group	End Item Price Group Mix Percentage
	6	602C	4,608			25
		602D	12,288			67
		602E	1,536	18,432	B	8
	12	602F	3,072			27
		602G	8,192	11,264	C	73
502X	1	502A	$9,360			20
		502B	18,000			40
		502C	18,000	45,360	D	40
	2	502D	56,160			36
		502E	102,000	158,160	E	64
	6	502F	28,080	28,080	F	100
840X	2	840A	$1,800			60
		840B	1,200	3,000	G	40

The end item price group mix percent will be used in a later sales family relationship. The conversion of the projected sales for a price group to quantities is a simple matter of division by the unit end item sales price. Note that (in the example below) a price group percentage mix is also calculated. This is used for sales family construction.

The basic pricing ground rules are:

A car or truck is $1.00

A case is $0.50

A box is $0.05

An electric car is $3.00

Unit Quantity and Mix Percentage Calculation
(dollars in thousands)

Product Group	Price Group	Price Group Projected Sales	Unit End Item Sales Price	Projected Price Group Required Quantity	Price Group Percentage Mix
602X	A	$ 11,264	$ 90.00	125,156	24
	B	18,432	78.00	236,308	46
	C	11,264	75.00	150,187	30
			Total	511,651	

Unit Quantity and Mix Percentage Calculation (continued)
(dollars in thousands)

Product Group	Price Group	Price Group Projected Sales	Unit End Item Sales Price	Projected Price Group Required Quantity	Price Group Percentage Mix
502X	D	$ 45,360	$ 75.60	600,000	22
	E	158,160	90.00	1,757,333	65
	F	28,080	78.00	360,000	13
			Total	2,717,333	
840X	G	$ 3,000	$234.00	12,821	100
			Total	12,821	

From the previously derived data, sales family structures can now be created for each product group. It should be recognized that The MTS Company knew at the start of this whole analysis that each product group had a different sales trend and should therefore be maintained separately. End items within a product group, however, have the same sales trend as the product group. A pictorial representation of the product group sales families is shown in Figure 3.5.

Note that since all mix percentages have been calculated (and included in Figure 3.5), the only item projections necessary for forecasting purposes are at the product group level. The annual projections are:

Product Group	Annual Projection
602X	511,651
502X	2,717,333
840X	12,821

There is an implied assumption in forecasting at the product group level that the mix percentages will remain constant across time. If there is a percentage variation, it will distort the disaggregation quantities at lower levels.

You probably noticed that Figure 3.5 is no longer a manufacturing view as previously shown for a product group. All variants are gone. The product group and price group levels are "pseudo" levels. That is, they do not exist as real tangible individual things that can be touched.

Another method of viewing the selection criteria for specific end items is shown below.

End Item Matrix

End Item	Number of Cases in Overpack				Case Handle	Customer Label			Case			
	72 #146	36 #122	12 #124	6 #126	#107	A #116	B #118	C #120	1 Per #142	2 Per #110	6 Per #112	12 Per #114
602A		X			X	X				X		
602B		X			X			X		X		
602C			X		X	X					X	
602D			X		X		X				X	
602E			X		X			X			X	
602F				X	X	X						X
602G				X	X		X					X
502A	X					X			X			
502B	X						X		X			
502C	X							X	X			
502D		X			X	X				X		
502E		X			X		X			X		
502F			X		X	X					X	
840A		X			X	X				X		
840B		X			X			X		X		

With the calculation of unit quantities, The MTS Company can now consider the construction of forecast data.

BUILDING THE FORECAST

Let us review the assumptions that have been made.

1. The mix percentages of end items and price groups within product groups is stable across time.
2. Sales families can be structured at the product group level.
3. It is beneficial to structure sales families, because a smaller number of forecast models need to be maintained (three at the product group level as opposed to 15 at the end item level).
4. Forecast models are derived initially from historical demand data and then adjusted by economic trends and management objectives.

At this point, let's assume that the following forecast models have been

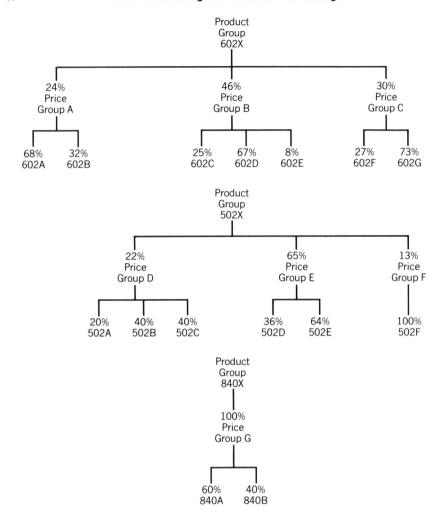

FIGURE 3.5 Sales family upper structure relationships.

adjusted and will be used to derive monthly (it actually could be for any period size, such as weekly or quarterly) quantities.

The Forecast Models

		Models		
Period	Month	602X	502X	840X
1	Jan.	1.05	1.10	0.98
2	Feb.	1.04	1.10	0.99
3	Mar.	1.01	1.05	0.99

The Forecast Models (continued)

Period	Month	Models 602X	502X	840X
4	Apr.	1.00	0.98	1.00
5	May	0.96	0.91	1.01
6	Jun.	0.94	0.90	1.04
7	Jul.	0.94	0.91	1.03
8	Aug.	0.96	0.94	1.01
9	Sep.	1.00	0.96	1.00
10	Oct.	1.02	1.00	0.99
11	Nov.	1.03	1.06	0.98
12	Dec.	1.05	1.09	0.98

Note that for every model (for 12 periods) the period quantities add up to 12.00. Once the model exists, it is then a simple matter to divide the annual forecast quantity by the number of periods (12) and then multiply it by the period model percentage. The calculations are shown below.

Quantity Distribution by Forecast Model

	602X	502X	840X
Annual Forecast Quantity	511,651	2,717,333	12,821
Average for a period to be multiplied by the model-percentage	42,638	226,444	1,068

Period	602X Model	602X Quantity	502X Model	502X Quantity	840X Model	840X Quantity
1	1.05	44,770	1.10	249,089	0.98	1,047
2	1.04	44,343	1.10	249,089	0.99	1,057
3	1.01	43,063	1.05	237,767	0.99	1,057
4	1.00	42,637	0.98	221,916	1.00	1,069
5	0.96	40,932	0.91	206,064	1.01	1,080
6	0.94	40,080	0.90	203,800	1.04	1,111
7	0.94	40,080	0.91	206,064	1.03	1,100
8	0.96	40,932	0.94	212,858	1.01	1,080
9	1.00	42,637	0.96	217,387	1.00	1,069
10	1.02	43,491	1.00	226,444	0.99	1,057
11	1.03	43,916	1.06	240,031	0.98	1.047
12	1.05	44,770	1.09	246,824	0.98	1,047
Totals	12.00	511,651	12.00	2,717,333	12.00	12,821

Although we now have what we feel is realistic projection data at the product group level, it may not be too useful for MPSP. Within MPP and MSP actual sales of end items may need to be blended to forecasted sales to increase the reliability of the projected quantities. It is not too practical to blend a thing, as a 602A, to a pseudo nonthing as a 602X. Therefore, the forecast must be exploded to lower levels.

The actual explosion logic, level by level, is illustrated in Appendix IV, "Conversion of Sales Data to Manufacturing Data."

At this point, we have reviewed last year's sales, applied some external adjustments to what the future sales might be, assembled future sales into sales families, applied forecast models to those sales families, and finally exploded the sales families to end item levels.

A forecast of end item requirements now exists for input to MPSP consisting of the following data.

Forecast Data (Statistical Projections)

End Item Forecast Quantities

Period	602A	602B	602C	602D	602E
1	7,307	3,438	5,149	13,798	1,648
2	7,237	3,405	5,100	13,667	1,632
3	7,028	3,307	4,952	13,272	1,585
4	6,958	3,275	4,903	13,141	1,569
5	6,680	3,144	4,707	12,615	1,506
6	6,541	3,078	4,609	12,353	1,475
7	6,541	3,078	4,609	12,353	1,475
8	6,680	3,144	4,707	12,615	1,506
9	6,958	3,275	4,903	13,141	1,569
10	7,098	3,340	5,002	13,404	1,600
11	7,167	3,373	5,050	13,515	1,616
12	7,307	3,438	5,149	13,798	1,648

End Item Forecast Quantities

Period	602F	602G	502A	502B	502C
1	3,626	9,805	10,960	21,920	21,920
2	3,592	9,711	10,960	21,920	21,920
3	3,488	9,431	10,462	20,924	20,924
4	3,454	9,337	9,764	19,529	19,529
5	3,316	8,964	9,067	18,134	18,134

End Item Forecast Quantities (*continued*)

Period	602F	602G	502A	502B	502C
6	3,246	8,778	8,967	17,934	17,934
7	3,246	8,778	9,067	18,134	18,134
8	3,316	8,964	9,336	18,732	18,732
9	3,454	9,337	9,565	19,130	19,130
10	3,523	9,524	9,964	19,927	19,927
11	3,557	9,618	10,561	21,123	21,123
12	8,626	9,805	10,860	21,720	21,720

End Item Forecast Quantities

Period	502D	502E	502F	840A	840B
1	58,287	103,621	33,382	628	419
2	58,287	103,621	33,382	634	423
3	55,638	98,911	30,910	634	423
4	51,928	92,317	28,849	641	428
5	48,219	85,723	26,788	648	432
6	47,689	84,781	26,494	667	444
7	48,219	85,723	26,788	660	440
8	49,809	88,549	27,672	648	432
9	50,869	90,433	28,260	641	428
10	52,988	94,201	29,438	634	423
11	56,167	99,853	31,204	628	419
12	57,757	102,679	32,087	628	419

CHAPTER FOUR

A MAKE-TO-
ORDER COMPANY

THE ENVIRONMENT OF THE MAKE-TO-ORDER COMPANY

The Make-to-Order (MTO) Company has been in business for about 20 years. They started out making a machine to work in a mining tunnel that would be able to move hard rock. This product, the 901, has been a good product line, although it is seasonal because it is used mostly above 5000 feet, and access to the mines is regulated by the seasons.

Product 902 was introduced later to handle coal mining. It is similar to the 901, but has a rather flat demand pattern. It has turned out to be the real money maker for the company.

Product 905 was introduced to handle the movement of soft rock. It has not worked out too well, and is being phased out.

A new product, the Model 910, is planned to handle the loading of salt. It is anticipated that this product will have a flat demand pattern once it is accepted by the customers.

These four products represent what The MTO Company produces. However, there is no such thing as a specific 901. There are too many options that a customer may elect such as engine type, altitude usage, emission control, transmission type, and others. As a result, seldom are two 901s produced that are exactly alike.

Orders are booked against a checklist that is called an "order entry option checklist," shown below. Note that "option" is being used to mean both option and variant.

Order Entry Option Checklist
(An "X" Indicates the Option That May Be Selected)

		Machine Model		
	901	902	905	910
A. Purpose of machine option				
Hard rock	X			
Coal		X		
Soft rock			X	
Salt				X
B. Engine type option				
Type EC	X	X	X	
Type ED	X	X		X
C. Engine use option				
Above 5000 ft. (P5)	X	X	X	
Below 5000 ft. (M5)	X	X	X	X
D. Emission control option				
Water bath	X	X	X	X
Heavy duty dry	X	X	X	X
Standard	X		X	
E. Transmission type option				
Type TA	X	X	X	X
Type TC	X	X	X	
Type TD	X	X		X
F. Bucket size option				
4 YD	X			X
6 YD	X			X
8 YD	X		X	
10 YD		X	X	
G. Bucket lip material option				
Alloy A		X		
ALloy B		X	X	
Alloy C			X	X
Custom Alloy	X			
Hard Steel	X		X	X
Magnesium	X			
H. Hydraulics option				
Self-extinguishing	X	X	X	
Standard	X		X	X

Order Entry Option Checklist (*continued*)
(An "X" Indicates the Option That May Be Selected)

	Machine Model			
	901	902	905	910
I. Tire type option				
Type WA	X			
Type WB	X		X	X
Type WC		X	X	X
Type WD		X		X

The company decided some time ago that, since every machine uses a bucket, buckets can be built to stock prior to a specific customer order. However, there are variations in buckets, such as size and shape. The bucket "customizing" to a specific customer order is done during the selection of the lip that goes on the bucket.

The MTO Company also has the following constraints.

1. Type ED engines have a nine month lead time.
2. All transmissions must be purchased in lots of 60 to 100. The transmission manufacturers are not interested in this company's business unless they have a volume order.
3. Lips are castings and have a six month lead time. Lips are not planned to be stocked except for service parts.

Every machine has the same basic construction. It consists of an engine/transmission assembly, a frame assembly, and a bucket assembly.

We will review the previous year's activity, develop projections for the future year, and finally define some of the input data necessary to manage the manufacturing process for the future year.

AN ANALYSIS OF THE PREVIOUS YEAR'S SALES ACTIVITY

Although the unit (model) volume is low for the MTO Company machines, the dollar value is significant. On the average, a machine sells for the following amount:

Average Machine Selling Prices

Machine	Price
901	$ 65,000
902	98,000
905	100,000
910	75,000

During the previous year, the following quantities of machines were shipped each month.

Unit Machine Volume for the Previous Year

Machine	1	2	3	4	5	6	7	8	9	10	11	12	Total
						Monthly Period							
901	6	8	10	16	6	6	6	5	5	5	6	6	85
902	40	40	40	40	40	40	40	39	38	41	42	40	480
905	12	11	10	9	8	8	7	7	7	6	6	6	97
910	0	0	0	0	0	0	0	0	0	0	0	0	0

If the machine quantity volumes are extended by the machine prices, the quantities can be converted to dollars as shown below. (See Table next page.)

The projection by marketing for the coming year is based on models (it actually is by models, by customer, and by country). This, unfortunately, is not the type of forecast data required by manufacturing due to the large number of available options.

DEVELOPING THE PROJECTIONS FOR THE FUTURE YEAR

It is anticipated at The MTO Company that these events will occur in the coming year.

1. Model 901 will continue to have about the same seasonal demand pattern.
2. Model 902, the mainstay for the company, will have a flat demand pattern.
3. Model 905 will phase out by June.
4. Model 910 will be introduced in February and will grow to about eight units per month.

This results in the following unit projection volumes.

Projected Unit Machine Volumes for the Future Year

Machine	1	2	3	4	5	6	7	8	9	10	11	12	Total
						Monthly Period							
901	6	8	10	16	6	6	6	5	5	5	6	6	85
902	40	40	40	40	40	40	40	40	40	40	40	40	480
905	5	4	3	2	1	0	0	0	0	0	0	0	15
910	0	1	2	3	4	5	6	7	8	8	8	8	60

Dollar Volume for the Previous Year
(All dollars in thousands)

Machine	1	2	3	4	5	6	7	8	9	10	11	12	Total
901	$ 390	$ 520	$ 650	$1,040	$ 390	$ 390	$ 390	$ 325	$ 325	325	$ 390	$ 390	$ 5,525
902	3,920	3,920	3,920	3,920	3,920	3,920	3,920	3,822	3,724	4,018	4,116	3,920	47,040
905	1,200	1,100	1,000	900	800	800	700	700	700	600	600	600	9,700
910	0	0	0	0	0	0	0	0	0	0	0	0	0
Total	$5,510	$5,540	$5,570	$5,860	$5,110	$5,110	$5,010	$4,847	$4,749	$4,943	$5,106	$4,910	$62,265

It is obvious that The MTO Company recognizes that, although Models 901 and 902 are stable from one year to the next, the Model 905 is in trouble. As a result, they have introduced the lower-priced Model 910, hoping to capture a new market in the salt industry. Although they know that they will not maintain their previous year's sales volume (as they had with the 905), they anticipate that the 910 will at least buffer the dollar decrease in sales.

In addition, the company plans to apply a 10% price increase to the 901 and 902, which will result in the following prices.

The unit model volumes extended by the selling prices result in the following projected dollar volumes.

Average Machine Selling Prices With Price Increases

Machine	Price
901	$ 71,500
902	107,800
905	100,000
910	75,000

The unit model volumes extended by the selling prices result in the following projected dollar volumes. (See Table next page.)

The MTO Company has a good idea at this point as to where their sales dollars will be coming from. They might, however, wish to perform a percentage variance analysis to relate the previous year to the future year. (See Table page 62.)

The MTO Company recognizes that costs have increased more than 3%, but the previous year was sort of lean. They are trying to recover and get back into the running with new products. They are satisfied with the 3% increase in sales, since they recognize that their potential big money maker, the Model 905, turned out to be a loser.

All of the projections developed by Marketing have been on models. Manufacturing, unfortunately, does not forecast the demand on models.

You will now begin to see why both a make-to-stock and a make-to-order company are being illustrated. The analysis of the input data for a MTO company is similar to, but not quite the same, as that previously reviewed for a MTS company.

Projected Dollar Volumes for the Future Year
(All dollars in thousands)

Machine	Monthly Period												Total
	1	2	3	4	5	6	7	8	9	10	11	12	
901	$ 429.0	$ 572.0	$ 715.0	$1,144.0	$ 429.0	$ 429.0	$ 429.0	$ 357.5	$ 357.5	$ 357.5	$ 429.0	$ 429.0	$ 6,077.5
902	4,312.0	4,312.0	4,312.0	4,312.0	4,312.0	4,312.0	4,312.0	4,312.0	4,312.0	4,312.0	4,312.0	4,312.0	51,744.0
905	500.0	400.0	300.0	200.0	100.0	0	0	0	0	0	0	0	1,500.0
910	75.0	150.0	225.0	300.0	375.0	450.0	525.0	600.0	600.0	600.0	600.0	600.0	5,100.0
Total	$5,316.0	$5,434.0	$5,552.0	$5,956.0	$5,216.0	$5,191.0	$5,266.0	$5,269.5	$5,269.5	$5,269.5	$5,341.0	$5,341.0	$64,421.5

Sales Dollar Percentage Change from the Previous Year to Projected Future Year

Monthly Period

	1	2	3	4	5	6	7	8	9	10	11	12	Total
Previous Year	$5,510.0	$5,540.0	$5,570.0	$5,860.0	$5,110.0	$5,110.0	$5,010.0	$4,847.0	$4,749.0	$4,943.0	$5,106.0	$4,910.0	$62,265.0
Projected Year	5,316.0	5,434.0	5,552.0	5,956.0	5,216.0	5,191.0	5,266.0	4,296.5	5,269.5	5,269.5	5,341.0	5,341.0	64,421.5
Percentage of Change	(0.04)	(0.02)	0	0.02	0.02	0.02	0.04	0.09	0.11	0.07	0.05	0.09	0.03

In the MTO company, the only data that Marketing provided to Manufacturing were the following model projections.

	Monthly Period											
Machine	1	2	3	4	5	6	7	8	9	10	11	12
901	6	8	10	16	6	6	6	5	5	5	6	6
902	40	40	40	40	40	40	40	40	40	40	40	40
905	5	4	3	2	1	0	0	0	0	0	0	0
910	0	1	2	3	4	5	6	7	8	8	8	8

These projections do not provide the required data for Manufacturing to run their business. For example:

1. Engine types ED have a nine-month lead time. How many should be ordered prior to actual customer bookings?
2. Bucket lips are castings and have a six-month lead time. How many of what type should be ordered to avoid missing a customer order?
3. Buckets are built to stock. Lips are added when a specific customer order is booked. What is the right quantity of buckets to have in stock?
4. Buckets and bucket lips are sold as service (replacement) parts. Will the inventory levels provide a realistic service level on these items?
5. Transmissions are purchased in quantities of 60 to 100. The lead time (purchasing) is two months. What is the lowest cost inventory level that can be maintained?

The first step performed by Manufacturing is to disaggregate the projected model quantities to option levels. This disaggregation process is illustrated in Appendix IV, "Conversion of Sales Data to Manufacturing Data."

All the explosions and calculations from Appendix IV result in the following projections for manufacturing. Note that the indicated quantities also include the forecasts for service part demand.

	Monthly Period											
Item	1	2	3	4	5	6	7	8	9	10	11	12
016T	19	26	32	51	19	19	19	16	16	16	19	19
018T	16	16	17	19	10	9	10	11	12	12	13	13
020T	44	44	45	46	47	47	49	52	54	54	54	54
022T	125	126	127	127	128	129	130	132	132	133	133	133
4AC	0	0	1	1	2	2	2	2	3	3	3	3
4CA	0	0	0	0	0	0	0	0	0	0	0	0

Monthly Period

Item	1	2	3	4	5	6	7	8	9	10	11	12
4HS	2	2	3	4	2	3	5	3	3	4	4	4
4MA	1	2	2	3	1	1	1	1	1	1	1	1
6AC	0	1	1	2	3	2	2	4	3	3	4	4
6CA	0	0	0	0	0	0	0	0	0	0	0	0
6HS	1	1	1	2	1	1	1	1	1	1	1	1
6MA	1	1	2	3	1	1	1	1	1	1	1	1
8AB	2	2	1	1	1	0	0	0	0	0	0	0
8AC	1	1	1	0	0	0	0	0	0	0	0	0
8CA	0	0	0	0	0	0	0	0	0	0	0	0
8HS	1	1	0	1	0	0	0	0	0	0	0	0
8MA	1	2	2	2	1	1	1	1	1	1	1	1
10AA	20	21	20	20	21	21	22	21	22	22	23	22
10AB	35	36	37	37	37	38	38	39	40	40	41	52
10AC	1	0	0	0	0	0	0	0	0	0	0	0
10HS	0	0	0	0	0	0	0	0	0	0	0	0
540H	4	6	6	9	6	7	8	9	10	10	10	10
640H	4	6	6	9	6	7	8	9	10	10	10	10
B4YD	3	5	6	10	6	7	8	7	8	9	9	10
B6YD	2	3	4	8	4	5	7	7	6	7	7	7
B8YD	8	7	5	4	3	1	3	2	3	2	1	2
B10YD	52	51	52	51	51	52	51	52	53	52	53	54
CHDD	7	7	8	6	6	6	6	6	6	6	6	6
CM5	13	14	14	15	12	12	12	12	12	12	12	12
CP5	10	8	9	9	7	6	6	6	6	6	6	6
CSTD	3	2	2	1	1	0	0	0	0	0	0	0
CWB	13	13	13	15	12	12	12	12	12	12	12	12
DHDD	9	9	9	11	9	9	9	8	8	8	9	9
DM5	16	18	20	23	20	21	22	23	24	24	24	24
DP5	12	12	13	15	12	12	12	11	11	11	12	12
DSTD	1	1	2	3	1	1	1	1	1	1	1	1
DWB	18	18	19	21	18	18	18	18	18	18	18	18
EC42	23	23	23	24	19	18	18	18	18	18	18	18
ED14	28	30	33	37	32	33	34	34	35	35	36	36
R901	6	8	10	16	6	6	6	5	5	5	6	6
RG902	40	40	40	40	40	40	40	40	40	40	40	40

	Monthly Period											
Item	1	2	3	4	5	6	7	8	9	10	11	12
RG905	5	4	3	2	1	0	0	0	0	0	0	0
RG910	0	1	2	3	4	5	6	7	8	8	8	8
TRA1	21	21	23	24	23	23	23	24	25	25	25	25
TRC2	16	17	17	19	14	14	14	14	14	14	14	14
TRD4	14	14	15	17	14	14	14	14	14	14	14	14

This concludes the review of business planning and forecast data management considerations. You should have noticed that although the derivation logic for MTS and MTO companies can differ widely, the end result should still be manufacturing data that can be utilized by MPP and MSP.

PART THREE

MASTER PRODUCTION PLANNING (MPP)

CHAPTER FIVE

GENERAL MPP
PHILOSOPHIES
AND CONSIDERATIONS

DIFFERING PHILOSOPHIES

The main purpose of MPP is to produce realistic item production plans for plant flow line scheduling and/or for input to MSP. The secondary purpose of MPP is to provide a management tool for estimating required future resources via resource requirements planning.

Two different philosophies exist regarding what the function content of MPP and MSP should be.

One philosophy states that MPP should be very general. It is a guideline, or a rough estimate as to what item production plans should be.

The second philosophy states that MPP should be as realistic as possible. If adjustments can be planned at the MPP level, then that is where they should be made, and they should not be deferred to MSP.

Admittedly the MPP level is more general than the MSP level. MPP planning is performed at a product family level with many items grouped into one or more families. The time horizon is usually rather long, like three to five years. The planning period (bucket size) is also usually large, usually in months, quarters, or semi-annual periods.

MSP planning is performed at the item level. The time horizon is shorter, like six months to a year. The planning period is also smaller, usually days, weeks or months. MSP also groups the item production planned quantities into order quantities according to pre-established lot sizing criteria.

While both MPP and MSP test plans against available resources, the key difference between the two philosophies is defining where adjustments should be made for an invalid plan. With the first philosophy, most adjustments are made in MSP. With the second philosophy, the adjustments that can be made in MPP are made there and any remaining adjustments indicated within MSP are made there.

Remember that the intent of MPSP as a whole is to produce plans that will satisfy anticipated demand while remaining within management guidelines, such as production targets and available resources. The "right philosophy" for any one company is the one that accomplishes the MPSP objective in the easiest way.

BUCKET SIZE CONSIDERATIONS

It is very common for the following types of bucket sizes (planning periods) to exist for various types of data for any one MPSP system.

Forecast input data
  1st Year in Months
  2nd Year in Quarters
  3rd Year as Semiannual Quantities
  4th and 5th Years as Annual Quantities
Actual sales data input
  No buckets used. The data are structured by item identification (part number), ship date (as June 18, 19XX) and a quantity.
MPP processing
  1st and 2nd years in quarters
  3rd, 4th and 5th years in semi-annual quantities
MSP processing
  One year of monthly quantities

The bucket sizes may vary across the horizon for any function. In addition, the bucket size and horizon may vary between functions.

The simplest approach is obviously not to do what was shown above. Make all buckets in weeks and make all horizons equal to five years. This is a simple approach, but not too practical since a lot of data would be maintained that has little usefulness. Who cares what the plans are in *week* 59? A more important consideration is, "What is the impact of our probable production plan on our available resources in *year* five? Do we need more floor space, more people, more machines, or what?"

A second approach is to maintain all data within the computer system as indicated above, but display it on terminals and reports in the realistic, practical bucket sizes and horizons as required by a user for the particular function. This has the disadvantage of requiring the computer system to set aside huge amounts of storage positions.

Possibly the most practical (but not necessarily the easiest) approach is to define and maintain by function, the correct bucket sizes and horizons that are needed by that function. This means that during start up of an MPSP system, a potential user must know what is required. It also means that conversion routines are necessary. For example, let's convert monthly periods into weekly periods. How many weeks are in a month? It is not four. A simple four-four-five algorithm is shown below.

Month	Weeks
1	4
2	4
3	5
4	4
5	4
6	5
7	4
Etc.	Etc.

Although simple, this algorithm gives strange answers without good reasons for those answers. Consider an MPP item production plan that says to make 40 items per month for a year. This data is sent to MSP, where it is converted to weekly quantities as shown below.

Month	Conversion	Week	Quantity
1	4	1	10
		2	10
		3	10
		4	10
2	4	5	10
		6	10
		7	10
		8	10
3	5	9	8
		10	8
		11	8
		12	8
		13	8

(continued)

Month	Conversion	Week	Quantity
4	4	14	10
		15	10
		16	10
		17	10

We obviously did not plan to make 10 items in some weeks and 8 in other weeks. We had a flat plan of 40 per month and would like a realistic plan per week. We could have multiplied 40 times 12 months to get 480 and then divided by 52 weeks equaling about 9 per week. This is not so easy if the plan is not flat, and it usually isn't.

In addition, you should account for holidays and/or summer vacation plant shutdowns. This makes the conversion from weeks or months to days even more complicated. An approach that works well in solving this conversion problem is an extension of the typical shop calendar (which counts workdays sequentially) as shown below.

SHOP CALENDAR

Calendar Month	Calendar Day	Day of Week	Comment	Shop Day	Week End
Jan.	1	Sat.			
	2	Sun.			
	3	Mon.	Holiday		
	4	Tues.		1	
	5	Wed.		2	
	6	Thu.		3	
	7	Fri.		4	X
	8	Sat.			
	9	Sun.			
	10	Mon.		5	
	11	Tue.		6	
	12	Wed.		7	
	13	Thu.		8	
	14	Fri.		9	X
	15	Sat.			
	16	Sun.			
	17	Mon.		10	
	18	Tue.		11	
	19	Wed.		12	

(continued)

SHOP CALENDAR (continued)

Calendar Month	Calendar Day	Day of Week	Comment	Shop Day	Week End
Jan. (cont.)	20	Thu.		13	
	21	Fri.		14	X
	22	Sat.			
	23	Sun.			
	24	Mon.		15	
	25	Tue.		16	
	26	Wed.		17	
	27	Thu.		18	
	28	Fri.		19	X
	29	Sat.			
	30	Sun.			
	31	Mon.		20	
Feb.	1	Tue.		21	
	2	Wed.		22	
	3	Thu.		23	
	4	Fri.		24	X
	5	Sat.			
	6	Sun.			
	7	Mon.		25	
	8	Tue.		26	
	9	Wed.		27	
	10	Thu.		28	
	11	Fri.		29	X
	12	Sat.			
	13	Sun.			
	14	Mon.		30	
	15	Tue.		31	
	16	Wed.		32	
	17	Thu.		33	
	18	Fri.		34	X
	19	Sat.			
	20	Sun.			
	21	Mon.	Holiday		
	22	Tue.		35	
	23	Wed.		36	

(continued)

SHOP CALENDAR (continued)

Calendar Month	Calendar Day	Day of Week	Comment	Shop Day	Week End
Feb. (cont.)	24	Thu.		37	
	25	Fri.		38	X
	26	Sat.			
	27	Sun.			
	28	Mon.		39	
Mar.	1	Tue.		40	
	2	Wed.		41	
	3	Thu.		42	
	4	Fri.		43	X
	5	Sat.			
	6	Sun.			
	7	Mon.		44	
	8	Tue.		45	
	9	Wed.		46	
	10	Thu.		47	
	11	Fri.		48	X
	12	Sat.			
	13	Sun.			
	14	Mon.		49	
	15	Tue.		50	
	16	Wed.		51	
	17	Thu.		52	
	18	Fri.		53	X
	19	Sat.			
	20	Sun.			
	21	Mon.		54	
	22	Tue.		55	
	23	Wed.		56	
	24	Thu.		57	
	25	Fri.		58	X
	26	Sat.			
	27	Sun.			
	28	Mon.		59	
	29	Tue.		60	

(continued)

SHOP CALENDAR (continued)

Calendar Month	Calendar Day	Day of Week	Comment	Shop Day	Week End
Mar. (cont.)	30	Wed.		61	
	31	Thu.		62	
Apr.	1	Fri.		63	X
	2	Sat.			
	3	Sun.			
	4	Mon.		64	
	5	Tue.		65	
	6	Wed.		66	
	7	Thu.		67	
	8	Fri.		68	X

If we use the previous example of a flat plant of 40 per month and we wish to change it to the correct quantity per week, then we could use the following logic with the shop calendar.

40 are planned for January
January has 20 shop days
40 divided by 20 equals 2 per day
Week 1 has 4 days times 2 equals 8
Week 2 has 5 days times 2 equals 10
Week 3 has 5 days times 2 equals 10
Week 4 has 5 days times 2 equals 10
19 shop days have been consumed out of the 20
The remaining day (for a quantity of 2) overflows to February

The spread for the January planned quantity would appear as follows.

					Week								
Month	1	2	3	4	5	6	7	8	9	10	11	12	13
Jan.	8.0	10.0	10.0	10.0	2.0								

Repeating the process for February and March would yield the following results. February has 19 days and March has 24 days.

	Week												
Month	1	2	3	4	5	6	7	8	9	10	11	12	13
Jan.	8.0	10.0	10.0	10.0	2.0								
Feb.					8.4	10.5	10.5	8.4	2.1				
Mar.										6.8	8.5	8.5	8.5	6.8
Total	8.0	10.0	10.0	10.0	10.0	11.0	11.0	8.0	9.0	9.0	9.0	9.0	7.0

The resultant weekly plan is not flat, but it is realistic. Weeks 1 and 8 had holidays, and therefore planned production should be less than for full weeks. February was a short month (in terms of days) so more must be planned per week than for a long month such as March, if monthly plans are to be met.

The advantage of this approach is that it works for all types of plans, not only those that are flat. It does have a key disadvantage; it requires that up-front work be done to define the shop calendar. The calendar should be reasonably firm. If it changes every month (eg., if holidays are added and/or deleted) then planned production quantities will vary and the total plan will appear nervous.

Additional flexibility is offered by the shop calendar concept in that the increment of time can be a work shift instead of a day. This will allow a production plan to be doubled on a day when two shifts are planned instead of one.

MULTIPLE PLAN CONSIDERATIONS

Most companies will want to deal with several types of plans at a product family level.

In December, a company will establish a base plan for each product family for the coming year. This base plan says, based on anticipated demand and planned production, here is what we think will ship and when. This base plan is often used for budget preparation for the coming year.

Company management may also wish to move the business in a particular direction. For example, let's say that 70% of the profit comes from standard products that have a 10% profit margin and 30% of the profit comes from customized products that have a 30% profit margin. A simplified summary of this situation is illustrated below.

Group	Cost of Goods	Profit Percentage	Profit
Standard	$700,000	10	$70,000
Custom	100,000	30	30,000
Totals	$800,000		$100,000

For this company, let's say that the total of $100,000 profit is acceptable, but they would like the profit source to be equally divided (50–50) between standard and customized products. If this could be accomplished, then the summary would change to this picture.

Group	Cost of Goods	Profit Percentage	Profit
Standard	$500,000	10	$ 50,000
Custom	167,000	30	50,000
Totals	$667,000		$100,000

Note that if this could be accomplished, the total profit remains the same, but the cash outflow is reduced from $800,00 to $667,000.

To accomplish a goal as described above, management will frequently set desired production targets. In this example they wish to manually direct resources away from standard products and apply them to custom products. The desired production target for a product family may therefore be used as a guideline for establishing the base plan for the coming year.

Another type of plan is the operational plan. This is the plan that is currently being used by MSP. Frequently a company will want to compare the operational plan to any of the other plans. This implies a reaggregation of the MSP item orders back to a product family level in order to do the comparison.

The development plan (the third type of plan) is the one that is being worked on now to develop the operational plan for next month. This is a temporary plan that exists only until it is used as the operational plan.

Let's consider how these various plans are used. Effectivity start/stop dates are associated with every plan for every family. The company builds a base plan for 19X2 on December 10, 19X1. The base plan has a start date of January 1, 19X2 and a stop date of December 31, 19X2. On December 20th, the company rolls the base plan data to the development plan. Additional managerial reviews and adjustments are made. The development plan data is rolled to the operational plan with a start of January 1, 19X2 and a stop of January 31, 19X2.

During January, the plant works against the operational plan. Meanwhile, demand is not happening exactly as predicted and production also varies due to machine breakdowns, illnesses, and so forth.

A new development plan is constructed. It is compared to the base plan and the aggregated MPS orders that were created from the operational plan.

When differences are understood and resolved, the development plan becomes the February operational plan.

A key test that takes place for the development of all plans is resource testing. Even production targets should be resource tested to insure that these quantities per period can actually be produced.

CMLT TIME FENCE CONSIDERATIONS

The CMLT is the Cumulative Material Lead Time, which is the total duration required to obtain all parts/materials and produce the product. It is not the same as the Cumulative Manufacturing Lead Time, which does not include the acquisition of parts/materials.
   Consider this situation.

	Month					
	1	2	3	4	5	6
Production target	50	50	50	60	60	60
Initial production plan	30	40	50	60	60	60

The CMLT is two months. Although manufacturing takes place within the production target period, the material/components must be ordered two months ahead of time.

	Month							
	11	12	1	2	3	4	5	6
Production target			50	50	50	60	60	60
Initial production plan			30	40	50	60	60	60
Order plan (for material)	30	40	50	60	60	60		

It is now period one. A new order comes in for a quantity of 10 to be shipped in period two. At first glance, we might assume that since the production plan calls for 40 and the production target is 50, we can raise the plan from 40 to 50. We actually could raise the plan, but we would not ship the product on time since we did not order the parts in period 12 for the additional 10 units. This CMLT is a time fence that controls where adjustments can be made.

INPUT DATA BLENDING CONSIDERATIONS

The management or manipulation of input data actually falls within the sub-MPSP function of demand analysis. By now you have noticed, however, that demand analysis is not treated as an independent subfunction. Demand analysis is the management of input data to MPP and MSP to improve accuracy and to calculate any additionally required data elements, such as net demand.
   Since there are many ways that demand can be managed and since demand

analysis can vary as related to MPP versus MSP, the subfunction is discussed within the major topics of MPP and MSP.

In MPP, the demand that is utilized may initially be gross forecast demand at a product family level. Or, it may be at an item level and have to be aggregated to a family level. These approaches imply that

1. The forecast is reasonably accurate
2. The company has inventory under control and does not have to perform a netting calculation

More often than not, the above two situations do not exist, and a company will elect to do one of the following:

1. Use forecast data, and net them to available inventory.
2. Use actual sales data, and net them to available inventory.
3. Use some mix or blend of forecast data and actual sales data, and net them to available inventory.

The decision logic as to which of the above possible choices would be used is almost intuitive. There are tools available, such as methods to measure forecast error, but the final decision is still usually made on an intuitive basis. It is what top management "feels" is the most realistic choice.

In a very general sense, it can be said that most make-to-stock companies will build to the forecast, and most make-to-order companies will build to the actual sales data. However, it is very difficult, in actual practice to clearly classify a company into one of these two categories such as Make To Order.

Many make-to-order companies will build service parts to stock. If they built purely to actual sales, they could have either very large inventories or very long lead times (from order placement to shipment) due to long purchase-item lead time requirements. In theory, it is nice to neatly categorize any given company into a specific grouping, as make to stock or make to order, but in actual practice this grouping is difficult to perform.

Let us make some assumptions before we discuss blending.

1. We knew the desired level of control that manufacturing wanted in MPP, so we already exploded all sales families to the correct level.
2. We knew that for an item that was part of an assembly and also sold as a service part, two inventories would be required—a sales inventory for the service part and an MRP inventory for the assembly component. (This is necessary to prevent double netting, that is, once in MPSP and once in MRP).

The decision of which items to control by MPP (sometimes called master level items or MLIs) is often based on one or more of the following criteria:

1. The item is a high-cost end item or component. Management wants it to be controlled by MPP to insure that inventory levels are at a minimum but that no potential sales are missed.

2. The item is a long lead time component of an end item. If the quoted delivery cycle (from order placement to order shipment) for the end item is two months, but the component has a six-month purchase lead item, then that component (if it is significant to the product) could be selected as an MLI.

3. The item is a common assembly (or major component) that is used in every one of the different end items that are sold. A practical way to build this assembly might be on a flow line that is controlled by a daily, weekly, or monthly production rate schedule. The schedule is not related to a specific end item as a shop work order might be.

4. The item has a history of being a problem item with constant production overages or shortages. Additional control can be imposed by making the item an MLI

An MTO company might decide that the level of control should be at the option level. Another company with only a few options per model might elect to use models as MLIs. Remember that whatever level is used, all data for netting and blending must be at the same level for the item.

Blending is the process of combining multiple sources of data for an item to improve the accuracy of the data. If we only want to use forecast data to calculate net item demands, you might assume that we do not blend. You would be right in theory, however, in an actual computer program, blending is almost always performed.

Refer to Figure 5.1. The logic inputs are forecast data and actual sales data. One of these may not actually exist (the fields or records may be blank), or the data accuracy of one of these two data sets may be highly questionable.

The first step is to select the data type to be used for blending. If "Forecast Data Only" was selected, actual sales data is set to zero. If "Actual Sales Data Only" was selected, forecast data is set to zero.

The second step is to blend. Whatever type of blending is used, the blending process always occurs even though you may simply be blending a valid quantity against a zero quantity.

There are many theoretical ways to blend such as:

1. For each period, use the greater of forecast data or actual sales data.

2. For a specific period (period five for example) blend the actual sales to the forecast in period five, then four, then three, then two, and then finally one.

3. For a specific period (such as period five) blend the actual sales to the forecast in period five, then six, then seven, and so on. (Note that this method implies that shipping dates are not quoted to a customer until blending has been completed).

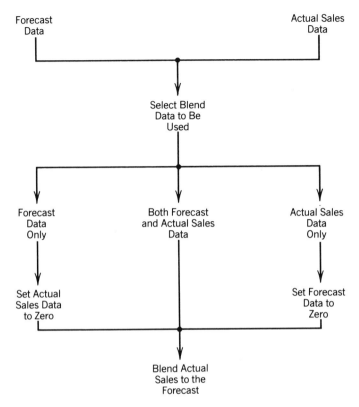

FIGURE 5.1   Basic blend logic.

4. Blend backwards to period one from period five, and then continue blending by going forward from period six.

5. For any of the previous approaches, control the blending by time fences to constrain the number of periods forward and backward in which blending can occur.

Let's walk through an example of blending using the second technique. The forecast for an item is 40 per period. So far no sales have been booked. The unconsumed forecast (forecast consumed by sales) is therefore 40 per period. The status is as shown below. The gross demand is the sum of the unconsumed forecast and actual sales.

	\multicolumn{6}{c}{Period}					
	1	2	3	4	5	6	Horizon Total
Forecast	40	40	40	40	40	40	240
Actual sales	0	0	0	0	0	0	0
Unconsumed forecast	40	40	40	40	40	40	240
Gross demand	40	40	40	40	40	40	240

Assume that an order is booked for a quantity of 55 in period three. The forecast quantity of 40 in period three is consumed, plus an additional 15 in period two.

	Period						
	1	2	3	4	5	6	Horizon Total
Forecast	40	40	40	40	40	40	240
Actual sales	0	0	55	0	0	0	55
Unconsumed forecast	40	25	0	40	40	40	185
Gross demand	40	25	55	40	40	40	240

An order is booked for a quantity of 35 in period five. Of the forecasted 40 in period five, 35 are consumed by sales and five remain unconsumed.

	Period						
	1	2	3	4	5	6	Horizon Total
Forecast	40	40	40	40	40	40	240
Actual sales	0	0	55	0	35	0	90
Unconsumed forecast	40	25	0	40	5	40	150
Gross demand	40	25	55	40	40	40	240

An order is booked for a quantity of 75 in period five. Only five remain available for consumption in period five, which leaves 70. Period four has 40 available for consumption, which leaves 30. Period three has no unconsumed forecast available, so we still have 30. Period two has 25 available, so we consume that, leaving five. Period one consumes the remaining five.

	Period						
	1	2	3	4	5	6	Horizon Total
Forecast	40	40	40	40	40	40	240
Actual sales	0	0	55	0	110	0	165
Unconsumed forecast	35	0	0	0	0	40	75
Gross demand	35	0	55	0	110	40	240

If this was the status within MPP when we wanted to use the gross demand to calculate net item demand, we might impose a further constraint called a demand time fence (DTF). Since we have no booked orders for the quantity of 35 in period one, should we really consider those 35 as demand? If we do, we are betting that sales will actually consume those 35 items. If we were conservative, we might establish a DTF between periods one and two. This would say that for period one, we only want to consider actual sales and not the unconsumed forecast as shown below.

	Period						
	1	2	3	4	5	6	Horizon Total
Forecast	40	40	40	40	40	40	240
Actual sales	0	0	55	0	110	0	165
Unconsumed forecast	0	0	0	0	0	40	40
Gross demand	0	0	55	0	110	40	205

A DTF can also be used to constraint the blending backward. If used for that purpose, we could not have blended into period one.

The above example consumed the forecast (with sales) backwards. We could also have consumed it forwards. Or backwards first, and then forward. Some companies use a planning time fence (PTF) to constrain the blending in the forward direction, just as the DTF could constrain the blending in the backward direction.

Now for a little reality. Of the different illustrated blending techiques, most companies will use the approach illustrated above. Almost no one uses the other techniques.

If we had used the first approach, it would have yielded the following gross demand data.

	Period						
	1	2	3	4	5	6	Horizon Total
Forecast	40	40	40	40	40	40	240
Actual sales	0	0	55	0	110	0	165
Gross demand	40	40	55	40	110	40	405

This approach was to use the greater of forecast or actual sales. Note that the gross demand has been inflated.

Which technique is best? It is the one with which management feels the most comfortable. *You should remember that this is a reflection of demand and not production*. The development of the item's production plan will contain a smoothing technique to level production to meet demand spikes.

CHAPTER SIX

PRODUCT FAMILY AGGREGATION

DETERMINING HOW ITEMS FIT INTO A FAMILY

As previously indicated, a sales family may have been exploded to almost any level. This level is the MLI and is now aggregated up to a product family level. The MLIs could be any of the following:

End items (products)
Assemblies
Models
Options
Service parts
Key components

In other words, a product family can be structured with any item that is significant to the company. The items may be grouped into a family because:

1. They use the same resources.
2. They have the same sales trends.
3. Or for any reason that causes a grouping that is significant to the company.

For example, consider a company that has the following types of products:

1. Products that are standard.

2. Products that are customized.

3. Products that have a high direct-labor consumption.

4. Products that have a high machine-hour consumption. (This group is often subdivided by key machine or work center groups or types.)

5. Products that are structured by their costs. (For example, high-cost items in family H, medium cost items in family M and low-cost items in family L.)

Many companies will not use just one of the above product family structuring approaches, but rather a combination of two or more. Consider this simple matrix example.

	Product Families										
Grouping Criteria	1	2	3	4	5	6	7	8	9	*	36
Standard product	X	X	X	X	X	X	X	X	X		
Custom product group A											
Custom product group B											X
High labor hours	X	X	X								
High machine hours W/C A				X	X	X					
High machine hours W/C B							X	X	X		
High machine hours W/C C											X
Cost group H	X			X			X				
Cost group M		X			X			X			
Cost group L			X			X			X		X

*Families 10 through 35 are not shown.

Adding another cost group or W/C (work center) grouping would have a major impact on the number of product families in the matrix, doubling the number of families from 36 to 72.

The product family structuring technique utilized by a company will vary based on how management would like to review the summarized data, and how the item production plans are to be derived.

There is one product family grouping rule that has additional implications. If items are grouped into product families based on similar sales trends (the same approach used to structure a sales family), then the product family production plans can be converted to item production plans by a process called percentage disaggregation.

For percentage disaggregation you must remember the mix percentage of every item in the family. After you smooth and adjust the family quantities across the horizon periods, the percentages can be used to calculate how much of any one item is planned for any specific period. It is important to understand how you might want to disaggregate a product family since it has a direct bearing on how the family is initially aggregated.

To illustrate the potential problems that might occur with disaggregation by percentage when items with nonsimilar sales trends are grouped in a product family, some percentage disaggregation tests were conducted against the same basic set of data. The actual test results are detailed in Appendix II. The test data and the summarization of the test results is described below. Note that since blending of actual sales data would not change the test results, the blending process has not been included in the tests.

These assumptions have been made.

1. The company is just starting to use MPSP, and their current inventory situation is not in total control.
2. A product family consisting of four items has been structured.

The four items (in the product family) are different in that:

1. Item 1 has seasonal demand.
2. Item 2 has flat demand, but has considerably larger quantities of period demand than the other items.
3. Item 3 is being phased out.
4. Item 4 is currently in design and is being phased in.

Test calculations are performed to determine:

1. Are inventory hedges built when required?
2. Do the large period quantities of item 2 distort the mix percentages of the other items?
3. Does item 3 phase out with a resulting zero inventory?
4. Does disaggregation cause nervousness? For example, does an item production plan from a period-one disaggregation have the same planned quantities (if nothing else changes) when time passes, as a period-two disaggregation?
5. Do any unusual (not acceptable to MSP) plans result from disaggregation?

The test data consist of the following information:

Gross Demand

Item	\multicolumn{13}{c}{Periods}
	1	2	3	4	5	6	7	8	9	10	11	12	Total
1	60	80	100	160	60	60	60	50	50	50	60	60	850
2	400	400	400	400	400	400	400	400	400	400	400	400	4800

(continued)

Gross Demand (continued)

Item	____	____	____	____	Periods								
Item	1	2	3	4	5	6	7	8	9	10	11	12	Total
3	50	40	30	20	10	0	0	0	0	0	0	0	150
4	0	10	20	30	40	50	60	70	80	80	80	80	600
Total	510	530	550	610	510	510	520	520	530	530	540	540	6400

Gross Demand Period Percentages

Item					Periods							
Item	1	2	3	4	5	6	7	8	9	10	11	12
1	0.12	0.15	0.18	0.26	0.12	0.12	0.12	0.10	0.10	0.10	0.11	0.11
2	0.78	0.75	0.73	0.66	0.78	0.78	0.77	0.77	0.75	0.75	0.74	0.74
3	0.10	0.08	0.05	0.03	0.02	0	0	0	0	0	0	0
4	0	0.02	0.04	0.05	0.08	0.10	0.11	0.13	0.15	0.15	0.15	0.15

Gross Demand Horizon Percentages

Item	6-Month Horizon	12-Month Horizon
1	0.15	0.13
2	0.75	0.75
3	0.05	0.02
4	0.05	0.10

Available Inventory

Item	Quantity
1	30
2	800
3	10
4	0

Net Demand

Item					Periods								
Item	1	2	3	4	5	6	7	8	9	10	11	12	Total
1	30	80	100	160	60	60	60	50	50	50	60	60	820
2	0	0	400	400	400	400	400	400	400	400	400	400	4000

(continued)

Net Demand (*continued*)

Item	Periods												Total
	1	2	3	4	5	6	7	8	9	10	11	12	
3	40	40	30	20	10	0	0	0	0	0	0	0	140
4	0	10	20	30	40	50	60	70	80	80	80	80	600
Total	70	130	550	610	510	510	520	520	530	530	540	540	5560

Net Demand Period Percentages

Item	Periods					
	1	2	3	4	5	6
1	0.43	0.62	0.18	0.26	0.12	0.12
2	0	0	0.73	0.66	0.78	0.78
3	0.57	0.31	0.05	0.03	0.02	0
4	0	0.07	0.04	0.05	0.08	0.10

Net Demand Horizon Percentages

Item	6-Month Horizon	12-Month Horizon
1	0.21	0.15
2	0.67	0.72
3	0.06	0.02
4	0.06	0.11

The test descriptions and results are shown below.

1. Net demand period percentages applied to cumulative family net demand variances with an inventory build-up/runoff calculation.

   Plans a negative item production plan on item 4 (which is being phased out) as well as other items when a demand spike occurs (as in period three).

2. Net demand period percentages applied against period net demand family variances.

   The resulting item production plans have no relationship to net demand. Item 3 is overplanned. Item 2 is underplanned.

3. Net demand horizon percentages applied against period net demand family variances.

Plans negative quantities on item 3 which is being phased out.

4. Gross demand period percentages applied to cumulative family net demand variances with an inventory build-up/runoff calculation.

Plans negative quantities on item 3, which is being phased out.

5. Gross demand period percentages applied against period net demand family variances.

Distorts item production plan quantities. For example, item 3 requires a quantity of 140 to be produced prior to phase out, yet this method plans for a quantity of 177 to be produced.
The item production plans for items 1 and 4 will result in a stockout.

6. Gross demand period percentages applied against period gross demand family variances.

Builds additional inventory instead of reducing the existing on hand inventory.
Plans for a stockout (production cannot meet demand) on item 4 in period four.

7. Gross demand horizon percentages applied against period net demand family variances.

Plans negative quantities for item 3.

8. Gross demand horizon percentages applied against family production plan quantities.

The developed item production plans have no relationship to reality (demand). This approach generates stockouts on all items.

9. Gross demand horizon percentages applied against period gross demand family variances and adjusted by inventory.

Plans negative quantities.

A comparison analysis of the various types of data that were used for testing, and the resulting test problems is shown on the next page.

Data Used for the Calculations	Test Methods								
	1	2	3	4	5	6	7	8	9
Period net demand percentage	X	X							
Horizon net demand percentage			X						
Period gross demand percentage				X	X	X			
Horizon gross demand percentage							X	X	X
Cumulative family variance	X			X					
Period net demand variance		X	X		X		X		
Period gross demand variance						X			X
Inventory adjustments									X
Family production plan quantity								X	
Problems with the Test Methods									
Plans negative quantities	X		X	X			X		X
Plans stockouts		X			X	X		X	
Plans distortion	X	X			X			X	
Plans an inventory increase						X			

The detail calculations for each of the tests is illustrated in detail in Appendix II.

The purpose of the above section is to illustrate that if percentage disaggregation is planned for use in developing item production plans from family production plans, then the items within the family should have virtually identical demand patterns (and therefore mix percentages) from one period to the next.

AGGREGATION DATA

It is easy to think of aggregation as the process of taking all item demands for a period and adding them together for a family period demand. Often, however, the process is more complex.

The family itself may be thought of as a simple product structure relationship. In fact, many product family structure relationships are maintained by a typical bill-of-material software package.

If we can assume that a structure relationship exists (as with the four items in one family in the previous percentage disaggregation example), we can now examine those data elements that a company might want to aggregate.

Many companies wish to manage family production plans with cost and sales dollars as well as quantities (of units). The item dollar values therefore are aggregated to a family level. It should be recognized that although an initial dollar aggregation can be very precise, it tends to become more general as the plan is managed. For example, assume the following four items in a family.

Item	Unit Cost	Period 1		Period 2		Period 3	
		Quantity	Cost	Quantity	Cost	Quantity	Cost
1	$22.00	60	$1320.00	80	$1760.00	100	$2200.00
2	10.00	400	4000.00	400	4000.00	400	4000.00
3	14.00	50	700.00	40	560.00	30	420.00
4	35.00	0	0	10	350.00	20	700.00
Family level		510	$6020.00	530	$6670.00	550	$7320.00
Average item cost/period			$11.80		$12.58		$13.31

The production planner decides that he or she wishes to level production to a smooth 530 per period, and 20 from period three are moved ahead to period one.

What is the cost impact on period three? The reduction could be 20 times $13.31, or $266.20. In actuality however, maybe the 20 that were moved did not represent an equal mix of all four items. Maybe only 20 item 4s were moved, which would represent a cost shift of 20 times $35.00, or $700.00.

The message in this discussion on costs is that the usage of costs (or sales dollars) at a family level is a general guideline only. The only time that it is truly accurate is directly after an aggregation. Also note that you would probably never see cents shown in costs. In fact, the dollars would probably be rounded to thousands.

The rounding-to-thousands capability does not only apply to costs. Many systems will permit the user to enter (XXX,000) or (000,000) to indicate how many low-end digits should be rounded. The number 1,682,491,822 at a family level will probably be managed by using 1,682.

Later in family plan management, you will see that an item production plan consists of item net demand plus item adjustments (if mix percentage disaggregation is not used). Item adjustments are the build ahead or hedge records entered by the production planner to smooth the spikes out of the production plan. These item adjustments could appear as follows:

(Item 2) Period	Period Hedge Records	Meaning
1	+ 140	Build an extra 140 early
2	+ 220	Build an extra 220 early
3	− 50	Consume 50 that were built early
4	− 110	Consume 110 that were built early

(*continued*)

(Item 2) Period	Period Hedge Records	Meaning
5	− 10	Consume 10 that were built early
6	− 10	Consume 10 that were built early
7	− 20	Consume 20 that were built early
8	− 20	Etc.
9	− 30	
10	− 30	
11	− 40	
12	− 40	

The above example is for item 2. The hedge records or adjustments for all items in the family must be aggregated period by period to develop family adjustments. Note that the adjustments at an item level are also maintained and utilized in MPP.

The item backlog is the quantity of sales for an item that has been booked, but not yet shipped. The item backlog (or actual sales) is blended to the item forecast, producing an item gross demand (or blended item gross demand). This is the company's best guess of what they think the demand will be. The item gross demand is aggregated period by period to family gross demand.

When item hedge records were constructed (as in the example for item 2 previously shown) another calculation was performed which was preparing the cumulative total of those hedge records. This cumulative is sometimes referred to as item-planned held inventory. Let's expand the previous example.

(Item 2) Period	Period Hedge Records	Cumulative Hedge Records
1	+ 140	140
2	+ 220	360
3	− 50	310
4	− 110	200
5	− 10	190
6	− 10	180
7	− 20	160
8	− 20	140
9	− 30	110
10	− 30	80
11	− 40	40
12	− 40	0

Note that at the end of period one, we are planning to have a quantity of 140 held inventory to satisfy some future requirement. It is called planned held inventory, because the inventory may not actually exist. In Manufacturing we may well have built the extra 140, but Marketing (never known to pass up a sale) may have sold some of our 140. The item-planned held inventory is aggregated to a family-planned held inventory and also maintained in MPP at an item level. Item-planned safety stock and item on-hand inventory are also aggregated to family-planned safety stock and family on-hand inventory respectively.

Within the aggregation process, an item-available inventory is calculated. The calculation consists of the item on-hand inventory minus the item-planned safety stock minus the item-planned held inventory. The item available inventory is netted (subtracted from) against the item gross demand to produce item net demand, which is utilized in MPP as well as aggregated to family net demand.

Later on, as we perform the production planning process, we will want some comparison displays relating what we thought would happen to what actually happened. Therefore every aggregation is dated so that we can relate this one to the last one. We also need three additional elements of information for tracking purposes.

Item last ending inventory. The on-hand inventory on the previous aggregation.

Item last period sales. The sales that have been booked since the last aggregation.

Item last period receipts. The production receipts since the previous aggregation.

All three of the above are aggregated to the family level.

When the last MPP cycle took place, the resulting item production plans were released to MSP and converted to orders. Within this MPP cycle we might wish to review how our current development plan relates to those orders. We would like to decrease any wide variations, since we do not wish to create nervous plans (abrupt changes from one planning cycle to the next). The MSP orders are at an item level, so they too must be aggregated to a family level before they can be used as a comparison guideline.

The next chapter shows how the aggregated data are utilized.

CHAPTER SEVEN

PRODUCT FAMILY AND ITEM PLAN MANAGEMENT

THE BASIC PLAN MANAGEMENT LOGIC

Before we get into the details of product family or item plan management, let's consider a simple example of plan management that does not require disaggregation at the end.

First we will perform the initial functions you might do if MPSP were in a start-up mode. Then we will consider additional steps that might be taken as times passes and things happen or don't happen as planned.

Let's assume that you have completed the process of structuring product families. You had 800 end items that were identified as items to be master production planned. After the family structuring process, you had 40 families with about 20 items per family, on the average.

Management now directs your attention to product family 16 (PF16). They have set a production target of 20 per day. This is the desired rate at which production is performed at the most cost-effective rate. The system will calculate your period rates when necessary, as shown below.

Period	Daily Production Target	Shop Days Per Period	Period Production Target
1	20	20	400
2	20	20	400
3	20	24	480

(continued)

Period	Daily Production Target	Shop Days Per Period	Period Production Target
4	20	19	380
5	20	20	400
6	20	15	300
7	20	20	400
8	20	19	380
9	20	25	500
10	20	18	360
11	20	22	440
12	20	20	400

Note that only 12 periods are shown in order to keep the example simple.

Suppose you use your system to perform a variance test.

The system retrieves the gross demands for the items in PF16. Your company has elected to use unblended forecasts as item gross demands, so actual sales are not reflected in any calculations. PF16 is a small family with only four items. The data retrieved by the system are shown below.

Product Family 16 Gross Demand

	Family Items			
Period	1	2	3	4
1	60	400	50	0
2	80	400	40	10
3	100	400	30	20
4	160	400	20	30
5	60	400	10	40
6	60	400	0	50
7	60	400	0	60
8	50	400	0	70
9	50	400	0	80
10	50	400	0	80
11	60	400	0	80
12	60	400	0	80

The system next retrieves the available inventory for these four items so that net demand can be calculated. Since you have just implemented master production planning, you have not built any hedges (planned held inventory). The inventory data retrieved by the system is shown below. (Note that safety stock is also not included in these examples).

Product Family 16 Inventory Status

	Item			
	1	2	3	4
Previous period available inventory	30	800	10	0
Previous period production	0	0	0	0
Subtotal	30	800	10	0
Previous period gross demand	0	0	0	0
Balance on hand	30	800	10	0
Previous period cumulative hedge	0	0	0	0
Current period available inventory	30	800	10	0

The abundance of zeros in the above data is due to the assumption that we are in the start-up mode of our MPSP system.

Based on the previously retrieved gross demands and the current period available inventories, the system calculates net item demands as shown below.

Product Family 16 Item Net Demand

Period	Family Items			
	1	2	3	4
1	30	0	40	0
2	80	0	40	10
3	100	400	30	20
4	160	400	20	30
5	60	400	10	40
6	60	400	0	50
7	60	400	0	60
8	50	400	0	70
9	50	400	0	80
10	50	400	0	80
11	60	400	0	80
12	60	400	0	80

The system next totals, for each item and for each period, the net demand and the hedge records (item adjustments). Since we are in a start-up mode, all of the hedge records are zero. The result of this process is the creation of development item production plans. At this time our development item production plans are equal to the calculated net demands.

The system now totals the development item production plans to derive the development product family production plan.

Development Product Family 16 Total Production Plan

Period	Family Items				Family Total
	1	2	3	4	
1	30	0	40	0	70
2	80	0	40	10	130
3	100	400	30	20	550
4	160	400	20	30	610
5	60	400	10	40	510
6	60	400	0	50	510
7	60	400	0	60	520
8	50	400	0	70	520
9	50	400	0	80	530
10	50	400	0	80	530
11	60	400	0	80	540
12	60	400	0	80	540

The system calculates the period and cumulative variance of the production target quantities and the development product family production plan quantities.

Product Family 16 Variance Test

Period	Period Production Target	Development Family Production Plan	Period Variance	Cumulative Period Variance
1	400	70	330	330
2	400	130	270	600
3	480	550	−70	530
4	380	610	−230	300
5	400	510	−110	190

(continued)

Product Family 16 Variance Test (continued)

Period	Period Production Target	Development Family Production Plan	Period Variance	Cumulative Period Variance
6	300	510	−210	−20
7	400	520	−120	−140
8	380	520	−140	−280
9	500	530	−30	−310
10	360	530	−170	−480
11	440	540	−100	−580
12	400	540	−140	−720

It is obvious from the results of this variance test that you are in trouble with this initial plan. Aside from being short by 720 across the horizon, most of your periods are out of balance.

You go back to Management and explain that a production target of 20 per day will not satisfy demand.

Management decides to add a new machine to the production line. They give you a new production target of 23 per day.

Your period production targets are calculated as shown below.

Period	Daily Production Target	Shop Days Per Period	Period Production Target
1	23	20	460
2	23	20	460
3	23	24	552
4	23	19	437
5	23	20	460
6	23	15	345
7	23	20	460
8	23	19	437
9	23	25	575
10	23	18	414
11	23	22	506
12	23	20	460

You again request a variance test, and receive the following results.

Product Family 16 Revised Variance Test

Period	Period Production Target	Development Family Production Plan	Period Variance	Cumulative Period Variance
1	460	70	390	390
2	460	130	330	720
3	552	550	2	722
4	437	610	− 173	549
5	460	510	− 50	499
6	345	510	− 165	484
7	460	520	− 60	424
8	437	520	− 83	341
9	575	530	45	386
10	414	530	− 116	270
11	506	540	− 34	236
12	460	540	− 80	156

This variance test indicates that across a 12-period horizon, an extra 156 items will be produced. You decide to live with this, knowing full well that actual production and actual demand will change over what was planned as you move through time.

You still have, however, some problems with negative variances in individual periods. You wish to review the individual items to make adjustments. You could have prioritized the four items to a particular sequence for review. Instead, you use the system default, which provides the item plans for review in the horizon total quantity descending sequence, as shown below.

Sorted Development Product Family 16 Production Plan

	Family Items				
	2	1	4	3	Family Total
Horizon Total	4000	820	600	140	5560
Period					
1	0	30	0	40	70
2	0	80	10	40	130
3	400	100	20	30	550
4	400	160	30	20	610

(continued)

Sorted Development Product Family 16 Production Plan (continued)

	Family Items				
	2	1	4	3	Family Total
Horizon Total	4000	820	600	140	5560
Period					
5	400	60	40	10	510
6	400	60	50	0	510
7	400	60	60	0	520
8	400	50	70	0	520
9	400	50	80	0	530
10	400	50	80	0	530
11	400	60	80	0	540
12	400	60	80	0	540

The reason for sorting the items on the horizon total is because if you are going to make adjustments, you have elected to adjust the high-volume items first.

We had established that we wanted an item horizon total in a high-to-low sequence. Therefore, item 2 is the first item that is made available with an adjustment screen, as shown below.

Product Family 16 Adjustment Via Item 2

Period	Product Family Period Variance	Development Item Production Plan	Period Hedge Records	Cumulative Hedge Records	Adjustment Quantity
1	390	0	0	0	
2	330	0	0	0	
3	2	400	0	0	
4	− 173	400	0	0	
5	− 50	400	0	0	
6	− 165	400	0	0	
7	− 60	400	0	0	
8	− 83	400	0	0	
9	− 45	400	0	0	
10	− 116	400	0	0	
11	− 34	400	0	0	
12	− 80	400	0	0	

You decide that you may be able to fix the entire family problem with item 2, due to the excessive item 2 inventory causing zero net demand in periods one and two. You start to fix the problem in period four (closest in) with a debit and credit for a quantity of two. You change the data with these adjustments.

Product Family 16 Adjustments Via Item 2

Period	Product Family Period Variance	Development Item Production Plan	Period Hedge Records	Cumulative Hedge Records	Adjustment Quantity
1	390	0	0	0	
2	330	0	0	0	
3	2	400	0	0	+2
4	− 173	400	0	0	− 2
5	− 50	400	0	0	
6	− 165	400	0	0	
7	− 60	400	0	0	
8	− 83	400	0	0	
9	45	400	0	0	
10	− 116	400	0	0	
11	− 34	400	0	0	
12	− 80	400	0	0	

The system responds with the following display.

Product Family 16 Adjustments Via Item 2

Period	Product Family Period Variance	Development Item Production Plan	Period Hedge Records	Cumulative Hedge Records	Adjustment Quantity
1	390	0	0	0	
2	330	0	0	0	
3	0	402	2	2	
4	− 171	398	− 2	0	
5	− 50	400	0	0	
6	− 165	400	0	0	
7	− 60	400	0	0	
8	− 83	400	0	0	
9	45	400	0	0	

(continued)

Product Family 16 Adjustments Via Item 2 (continued)

Period	Product Family Period Variance	Development Item Production Plan	Period Hedge Records	Cumulative Hedge Records	Adjustment Quantity
10	− 116	400	0	0	
11	− 34	400	0	0	
12	− 80	400	0	0	

You decide that you now want to hedge the − 171 quantity in period four. You make the following adjustments.

Product Family 16 Adjustments Via Item 2

Period	Product Family Period Variance	Development Item Production Plan	Period Hedge Records	Cumulative Hedge Records	Adjustment Quantity
1	390	0	0	0	
2	330	0	0	0	+ 171
3	0	402	2	2	
4	− 171	398	− 2	0	− 171
5	− 50	400	0	0	
6	− 165	400	0	0	
7	− 60	400	0	0	
8	− 83	400	0	0	
9	45	400	0	0	
10	− 116	400	0	0	
11	− 34	400	0	0	
12	− 80	400	0	0	

The system responds with the following display.

Product Family 16 Adjustments Via Item 2

Period	Product Family Period Variance	Development Item Production Plan	Period Hedge Records	Cumulative Hedge Records	Adjustment Quantity
1	390	0	0	0	
2	159	171	171	171	

(continued)

Product Family 16 Adjustments Via Item 2 (continued)

Period	Product Family Period Variance	Development Item Production Plan	Period Hedge Records	Cumulative Hedge Records	Adjustment Quantity
3	0	402	2	173	
4	0	227	− 173	0	
5	− 50	400	0	0	
6	− 165	400	0	0	
7	− 60	400	0	0	
8	− 83	400	0	0	
9	45	400	0	0	
10	− 116	400	0	0	
11	− 34	400	0	0	
12	− 80	400	0	0	

You use the same process to make the following additional adjustments.

	Adjustment Number											
Period	1	2	3	4	5	6	7	8	9	10	11	Total
1					+56	+60	+83		+71	+34	+80	+384
2		(+171)	+50	+109								+330
3	(+2)											+2
4	(−2)	(−171)										−173
5			−50									−50
6				−109	−56							−165
7						−60						−60
8							−83					−83
9								+45				+45
10								−45	−71			−116
11										−34		−34
12											−80	−80

Note that although the 11 adjustments can be made individually as has been illustrated, they also could have been made with a single pass (single adjustment entry). All adjustments for all periods could have been entered at one time, but you would have had to do the arithmetic to calculate the adjustment quantities off line, which increases the error potential.

At the conclusion of all of your adjustment entries, the system provides the following display.

Product Family 16 Adjustments Via Item 2

Period	Product Family Period Variance	Development Item Production Plan	Period Hedge Records	Cumulative Hedge Records	Adjustment Quantity
1	0	384	384	384	
2	0	330	330	714	
3	0	402	2	716	
4	0	227	− 173	543	
5	0	350	− 50	493	
6	0	235	− 165	328	
7	0	340	− 60	268	
8	0	317	− 83	185	
9	0	445	45	230	
10	0	284	− 116	114	
11	0	366	− 34	80	
12	0	320	− 80	0	

You have met your objective to balance the family plan with item 2. However, recognize that you are now building ahead up to 716 item 2s in period three. This increases your on-hand inventory and therefore your inventory carrying costs. If we were dealing with a 36-month horizon, you probably would not want to build hedge records for all 36 months. Most companies would establish a hedging time fence of say six, nine, or 12 months. This time fence puts a control on how far into the future hedging is allowed. No one usually wants to build a huge quantity of an item today to cover a demand spike that may occur in three years.

Your management is satisfied with your adjustments, but they ask for the impact on inventory for the item (2) to which you made all of the adjustments.

The system retrieves and displays the following data.

Item 2 Inventory Projection

Period	Starting Balance on Hand	Development Item Production Plan	Total on Hand	Gross Demand	Ending Balance on Hand
1	800	384	1184	400	784
2	784	330	1114	400	714

(continued)

Item 2 Inventory Projection (continued)

Period	Starting Balance on Hand	Development Item Production Plan	Total on Hand	Gross Demand	Ending Balance on Hand
3	714	402	1116	400	716
4	716	227	943	400	543
5	543	350	893	400	493
6	493	235	728	400	328
7	328	340	668	400	268
8	268	317	585	400	185
9	185	445	630	400	230
10	230	284	514	400	114
11	114	366	480	400	80
12	80	320	400	400	0

This appears to be a reasonable plan to your management. You are staying within the production target. You are driving inventory down to zero. You have a plan that will meet the projected gross demand.

Now you would perform a resource requirements test on PF16, along with all of the other product families. Additional adjustments might be required as a result of the resource requirements testing.

Finally, when all adjustments have been made, the development item production plans are passed to MSP for conversion to orders.

Now, let's assume that everything that you planned for period one happened as planned. You are, however, at the end of period one and you want to replan, if it should be required. Note that the old period one has gone away and a new period 13 has been added at the end of period 12.

You request that your system perform the variance tests on all 40 families.

For PF16, the system retrieves the gross demands as shown below.

Product Family 16 Gross Demand

	Family Items			
Period	1	2	3	4
2	80	400	40	10
3	100	400	30	20
4	160	400	20	30
5	60	400	10	40
6	60	400	0	50

(continued)

Product Family 16 Gross Demand (continued)

Period	Family Items 1	2	3	4
7	60	400	0	50
7	60	400	0	60
8	50	400	0	70
9	50	400	0	80
10	50	400	0	80
11	60	400	0	80
12	60	400	0	80
13	70	400	0	80

The system next retrieves the available inventories as shown.

Product Family 16 Inventory Status

	Item 1	2	3	4
Previous period available inventory	30	800	10	0
Previous period production	30	384	40	0
Subtotal	60	1184	50	0
Previous period gross demand	60	400	50	0
Balance on hand	0	784	0	0
Previous period cumulative hedge	0	384	0	0
Current period available inventory	0	400	0	0

The system calculates the net item demands.

Product Family 16 Net Demand

Period	Family Items 1	2	3	4
2	80	0	40	10
3	100	400	30	20
4	160	400	20	30

(continued)

Product Family 16 Net Demand (continued)

	Family Items			
Period	1	2	3	4
5	60	400	10	40
6	60	400	0	50
7	60	400	0	60
8	50	400	0	70
9	50	400	0	80
10	50	400	0	80
11	60	400	0	80
12	60	400	0	80
13	70	400	0	80

The system next applied the hedge records. Since only item 2 had hedge records, the calculation for item 2 is the only one that is illustrated below.

Item 2 Development Production Plan Calculation

Period	Net Demand	Period Hedge Records	Item Production Plan
2	0	330	330
3	400	2	402
4	400	− 173	227
5	400	− 50	350
6	400	− 165	235
7	400	− 60	340
8	400	− 83	317
9	400	45	445
10	400	− 116	284
11	400	− 34	366
12	400	− 80	320
13	400	0	400

The system then totals the development item production plans to derive the development product family production plan.

Development Product Family 16 Total Production Plan

Period	Family Items 1	2	3	4	Family Total
2	80	330	40	10	460
3	100	402	30	20	552
4	160	227	20	30	437
5	60	350	10	40	460
6	60	235	0	50	345
7	60	340	0	60	460
8	50	317	0	70	437
9	50	445	0	80	575
10	50	284	0	80	414
11	60	366	0	80	506
12	60	320	0	80	460
13	70	400	0	80	550

The variance test is displayed next.

Product Family 16 Variance Test

Period	Period Production Target	Development Family Production Plan	Period Variance	Cumulative Period Variance
2	460	460	0	0
3	552	552	0	0
4	437	437	0	0
5	460	460	0	0
6	345	345	0	0
7	460	460	0	0
8	437	437	0	0
9	575	575	0	0
10	414	414	0	0
11	506	506	0	0
12	460	460	0	0
13	552	550	2	2

Since actual performance matched planned performance in period one, you would have expected the above results. No adjustments are necessary.

You perform the resource requirements test on the development family plan with all of the other families. After adjustments, you convert the development item production plans to operational item production plans and submit them to MSP.

Now, let's assume that production and demand did not occur as planned. After all, this is real life. Does it make the system nervous with excessive fluctuations? It may, but the nervousness is dependent on the probable error percentage of your gross demand numbers. If your demand numbers are realistic, your nervousness will be minimum. If your demand data are guesses, then expect your plans to have wide variations from one planning period to the next.

Let's assume that the following happened in period two.

	Production		Gross Demand	
Item	Planned	Actually Happened	Planned	Actually Happened
1	80	60	80	60
2	330	300	400	410
3	40	45	40	35
4	10	20	10	15

The above changes have an impact on your system's inventory calculations, which are shown below.

Product Family 16 Inventory Status

	Item			
	1	2	3	4
Previous period available inventory	0	784	0	0
Previous period production	60	300	45	20
Subtotal	60	1084	45	20
Previous period gross demand	60	410	34	15
Balance on hand	0	674	10	5
Previous period cumulative hedge	0	714	0	0
Current period available inventory	0	−40	10	5

Let us also assume that the original gross demand projections did not change at this time. If they had changed, then the steps that you would utilize would be very similar to those at the start up, except that you would have planned hedges in place.

You request that your system perform the variance tests.

For PF16, the system first retrieves the gross demands as shown below.

Product Family 16 Gross Demand

Period	1	2	3	4
3	100	400	30	20
4	160	400	20	30
5	60	400	10	40
6	60	400	0	50
7	60	400	0	60
8	50	400	0	70
9	50	400	0	80
10	50	400	0	80
11	60	400	0	80
12	60	400	0	80
13	70	400	0	80
14	80	400	0	80

The system next (after retrieving the available inventories) calculates the item net demands.

Product Family 16 Item Net Demand

	Family Items			
Period	1	2	3	4
3	100	440	20	15
4	160	400	20	30
5	60	400	10	40
6	60	400	0	50
7	60	400	0	60
8	50	400	0	70
9	50	400	0	80
10	50	400	0	80
11	60	400	0	80

(*continued*)

Product Family 16 Item Net Demand (continued)

Period	\multicolumn{4}{c}{Family Items}			
	1	2	3	4
12	60	400	0	80
13	70	400	0	80
14	80	400	0	80

The system next applies the hedge records to the net demand data. (Only item 2 is shown since it was the only item with hedge records.)

Item 2 Development Production Plan Calculation

Period	Net Demand	Period Hedge Records	Item Production Plan
3	440	2	442
4	400	− 173	227
5	400	− 50	350
6	400	− 165	235
7	400	− 60	340
8	400	− 83	317
9	400	45	445
10	400	− 116	284
11	400	− 34	366
12	400	− 80	320
13	400	0	400
14	400	0	400

The system accumulates all of the development item production plans to calculate the family plan.

Development Product Family 16 Total Production Plan

Period	\multicolumn{4}{c}{Family Items}				Family Total
	1	2	3	4	
3	100	442	20	15	577
4	160	227	20	30	437
5	60	350	10	40	460

(continued)

Development Product Family 16 Total Production Plan (continued)

Period	Family Items				Family Total
	1	2	3	4	
6	60	235	0	50	345
7	60	340	0	60	460
8	50	317	0	70	437
9	50	445	0	80	575
10	50	284	0	80	414
11	60	366	0	80	506
12	60	320	0	80	460
13	70	400	0	80	550
14	80	400	0	80	560

The system then provides you with the variance test results that you requested.

Product Family 16 Variance Test

Period	Period Production Target	Development Family Production Plan	Period Variance	Cumulative Period Variance
3	552	577	− 25	− 25
4	437	437	0	− 25
5	460	460	0	− 25
6	345	345	0	− 25
7	460	460	0	− 25
8	437	437	0	− 25
9	575	575	0	− 25
10	414	414	0	− 25
11	506	506	0	− 25
12	460	460	0	− 25
13	552	550	+ 2	− 23
14	437	560	− 123	− 146

Demand cannot be satisfied with this plan due to the negative cumulative variance. However, the quantity is small (25), and Management might elect to schedule a Saturday of work. Conversely, they might elect to ignore the negative variance and miss the potential sales quantity.

The negative variance in period 14 may or may not have adjustments made to compensate for it. If Management was reviewing a 36-month horizon instead of the 12 periods in our example, they would be looking for a trend. If demand was increasing for periods 15, 16, 17, 18 and so on also, then they would probably adjust the production target by adding personnel or machines.

The previous iterations should provide you with some perspective on how a product family may be managed. You will note that in the illustrated logic, all adjustments were made at the item (and not the family) level. Therefore, aggregation of item data to a family level takes place, but disaggregation of family data to the item level never takes place. This logic works equally well regardless of the criteria used for structuring a product family.

FAMILY PLAN MANAGEMENT

In the next sections, we will use the data that were aggregated in Chapter 6 together with the plan management logic just described.

The family production target is calculated as previously shown with a production target rate per day and a shop calendar that shows the shop days within any one period. This become a desired family production target against which the variances are calculated. It is not the development family production plan.

In the last planning cycle, adjustments were made to items. The adjustment have now (for this planning cycle) been aggregated to the family level. These are added (period by period) to the family net demand that exists now in order to create the initial development family production plan.

You will remember that with the previous plan management logic the planning technique attempted to drive inventory levels to zero. This is not necessarily desired by all companies. They will wish to drive inventory to some specific quantity on a particular date. This family desired inventory quantity and date, with the family on-hand inventory, the family gross demand and the initial development family production plan can be used to calculate a family projected on-hand inventory. The process of performing this calculation revises our initial development family production plan, since a planned inventory level in some future period can be viewed as another type of demand. A word of caution about using planned inventory levels at a family level: If you have 20 end items in the family, you really do not know how many of which items you are planning to have on hand in some future period.

One additional set of data is useful at this time. During the last planning cycle, you built a family development plan. When you adjusted it to your satisfaction, you released the item production plans to MSP. You also saved the family plan as the family operating plan. This is the family plan under which you are currently operating (at an item level). Now you retrieve this family operating plan and use it for comparison purposes.

You can now build a family plan management display screen with these data.

Family production targets
Development family production plan
Family operating plan

This screen should also display the calculated period and cumulative variances.

The production planner should be able to adjust the quantities in the development family production plan, which will cause the variances to be recalculated.

A projected inventory display is a very useful screen as a backup at the family level. The data needed for this display is the following.

Development family production plan
Family on-hand inventory
Family planned held inventory (hedges/build aheads)
Family planned safety stock
Family gross demand

This display indicates that if demand holds true and we release the development production plan, then this is what our family inventory picture will be, period by period.

The production planner can now perform the following steps.

1. Smooth the development family production plan quantities by staying within the production targets.
2. Compare the new plan to the last period's operating plan so that unnecessary plan nervousness is not introduced.
3. Peform an inventory projection.
4. Perform the resource requirements test on the development family production plan.
5. Make any additional adjustments based on the outcome of the resource testing.
6. Review the family production plans and inventory projections with management.
7. Upon management approval, release the family period variances to item plan management.

ITEM PLAN MANAGEMENT

The steps in performing item plan management are identical to those described in the basic plan management logic. The data needed to build the display screen are as follows:

Family period variances
Item net demand (as of now)
Item adjustments (from the last planning period)
Item planned held inventory
Shop calendar
Past period item production plan

The new item production plan is calculated from the net demand and adjustments. A daily production rate is calculated for reference purposes with the production plan and the shop calendar.

The planner enters adjustments in an attempt to eliminate any negative family period variances. These entries cause changes to be made to the family period variances, the item adjustments, the item planned held inventory (which is a cumulative total of the item adjustments), and the daily production rate.

Note that the past period's item production plan is used for comparison purposes to decrease unnecessary nervousness in planned quantities from one planning cycle to the next.

The planner steps through the items in the family until all negative family period variances are gone.

The new item production plans (net demand plus *all* item adjustments) can now be released to MSP.

COMPARISON DISPLAYS

There are comparison displays that many companies like to utilize to evaluate performance to date. However, a comparison implies relating some status of today's data against some reference data. That reference data is called a "base plan."

At the beginning of the year, a company will identify the family operating production plan, the family planned safety stock, the family on-hand inventory, and the family gross demand. These four records of information, along with a calculated family projected on-hand inventory are stored as the base plan. Frequently, budgets are set according to this base plan. It can be viewed in dollars as well as units. It is the reference point that can be measured against as the company progresses through the year. Two types of comparisons are made to the base plan—a base plan to actual data display and a base plan to development plan display.

At the close of each planning period, three elements of information have to be recorded at the item level and aggregated to the family level. These are the item on-hand inventory, the item sales for the period, and the item production receipts for the period. With this data, we can compare how sales are actually progressing against what we thought the gross demand would be when we stored the base plan. Likewise, we can compare planned to actual production and inventory.

When we initiated the base plan, we retrieved four data records, calculated a fifth, and stored all five. As a new development plan is created in a planning cycle, the same five data records (of the family development production plan) can be used for the second type of base plan comparison display.

Lastly, there is a third type of comparison display that does not involve the base plan. This comparison requires the aggregation of MSP item order quantities back to a family level and relating those to the family development production plan. This comparison can be the final check to insure that, at a family level, our new development plan is not causing nervousness on the orders already in MSP.

This text has treated MPP with the rationale that we wanted to perform all of the functions that we could at the MPP level before we passed the data to MSP.

PART FOUR

MASTER SCHEDULE PLANNING (MSP)

CHAPTER EIGHT

GENERAL MSP PHILOSOPHIES

PLAN VIA MPP, VIA MSP, OR VIA BOTH

The entire manufacturing function of MPSP covers:

An analysis of demand
Aggregation to a product family level
Smoothing and resource testing of families
Planning order quantities of items
Rough-cut capacity testing of item orders
Release of orders to MRP

Just because all the above logic exists within the total MPSP functional area does not mean that everyone will utilize it.

Company A has flow lines. They know the possible daily rates by which product can be produced on their flow lines. They build three different sizes of television sets, but 40 different end items are shipped due to private labeling and case variations.

When Company A analyzes demand, they reduce the forecasts for the 40 end items down to the three different chassis types. They use gross demand quantities only, with no netting to inventory, because they feel that they have their inventory under control. They smooth the period quantities with the flow line optimum rates. The rates are used to set up the plant to produce the three chassis to stock. This is how Company A performs MPP.

Company A also does MSP. Actual orders within a four-week frozen zone are released to the shops. The chassis is now treated as if it were a purchased assembly. The chassis, the case, the private labeling material, and the packing material are withdrawn from stock, and final assembly takes place.

Company A is a make-to-stock and assemble-to-order company. They did not use all of the possible functions available within MPSP. They used what they felt was necessary to provide for an effective plant operation.

Company B used to build forklifts. They made a profit of 15% over cost on every forklift that they sold. They also sold service parts (spares) for their forklifts. They made a profit of 350% over cost on service parts. They decided that since they had a variety of machine shops (which could make almost any kind of spare part) and since service parts were more profitable than forklifts, they would go 100% into the service parts business.

They received forecasts from distribution centers for the 4000 service parts that they sold. They calculated net demands for these parts, since on less-expensive parts they could have a two- or three-month supply on hand.

They grouped their item net demands into product families based on the type of work that had to be performed to make the parts. They smoothed their family period quantities after resource testing (if the resource requirements test was not passed).

Item production plans were then converted to order quantities. The lot size or order quantity for an item was based on set-up costs.

Planned order quantities were adjusted up and down depending on how actual sales were taking place. Company B is a make-to-stock company that wants to keep their inventory as low as possible without missing sales.

As you can tell, a pure make-to-order company would be entirely different. Master production schedule planning is a function that varies in usage according to the type of company and the needs of that company. It is not, for example, like an inventory accounting function. Almost everyone in manufacturing uses inventory accounting. And almost everyone says that available inventory is equal to the on-hand inventory minus allocations minus safety stock. There is very little that is "standard" in MPSP from one manufacturing company to the next.

MSP DEMAND

We have implied previously that the inputs to MSP were item production plans coming from MPP. Some people, however, will say that they do not want to do MPP. They want to analyze and blend demands. They want to build hedge inventories and they want to resource test. They say that they are doing master scheduling and not master production schedule planning. This is a play on words. The key thing that they are not using in MPSP is the product family capability, and that is okay if it works well for their operation.

The inputs that could come to MSP are similar to those for MPP, with a few additional ones.

Forecast data

Actual sales data

Blended gross demands

Net demands

Manually entered order quantities

Item production plans

And, similar to MPP, these inputs could be for any master level item (MLI): end items, models, options, service parts, major assemblies, or key components.

The differences between MPP and MSP are that in MPP we use large planning buckets across a long horizon and want to feel that our plan is achievable. IN MSP, we take some inputs, convert them to orders, and then release those orders to the shop. We want a high level of assurance that the plan is achievable. If we did not use MPP, then in MSP we could have inputs that would normally have gone to MPP, which we now could convert to orders and still have the same concerns about an achievable plan.

As we proceed, we will assume that MPP is in place, and we will use the resultant item production plans as our key input to MSP. This does not mean that the other possible MSP inputs are ignored. As companies manage master schedule orders, they would like to have some comparison data on the display screens to see how these orders relate to the original forecast and/or actual sales.

Also, features that were discussed in MPP, such as blending and hedging, will not be discussed again in MSP, even though MSP is where a company might elect to utilize those features.

CONVERSION—BUCKETS AND QUANTITIES

Many companies will want to convert the planning periods (buckets) that were used in MPP to something smaller in MSP. If MPP used quarters, then MSP might use months. IF MPP used months, then MSP might use weeks. As previously mentioned, the easiest way to do this is to convert to workdays and then roll workday quantities back to the desired period size.

The conversion process works very well when large quantities per period exist. Rounding errors become insignificant. But, what about when the planned quantity per month was two? There are 22 workdays this month. Do you want to calculate that 0.091 items should be produced each day? If there are four weeks in this month (with two days going into the fifth week), do you want to say that 0.455 of the item should be produced each week? Of course not! Calculations of that type border on the ridiculous. A more practical approach is to show the master scheduler the monthly requirement and let him or her decide to plan one in week two and one in week four.

However, when the quantities per period are large, the quantities from one period to the next vary, and a large number of items are involved, then the calculations are best performed with a computer.

Consider this example. The item production plan submitted to MSP is as follows.

| | Month | | |
	Jan.	Feb.	Mar.
Quantity	380	400	430

The workdays in each month are as follows.

| | Month | | |
	Jan.	Feb.	Mar.
Workdays	20	19	23
Day			
From	1	21	40
To	20	39	62

The quantity per day is as follows.

| | Month | | |
	Jan.	Feb.	Mar.
Quantity/month	380	400	430
Workdays	20	19	23
Quantity/day	19.00	21.05	18.70

The calculation to determine the quantity per week is shown below.

| Week | Workday | | Number of Days | Quantity/Day | Quantity/Week | |
	From	To			Calculated	Rounded
1	1	4	4	19.00	76.00	76
2	5	9	5	19.00	95.00	95
3	10	14	5	19.00	95.00	95
4	15	19	5	19.00	95.00	95

(continued)

	Workday		Number		Quantity/Week	
Week	From	To	of Days	Quantity/Day	Calculated	Rounded
5	20	24	1	19.00	19.00	
			4	21.05	84.20	
					103.20	103
6	25	29	5	21.05	105.25	105
7	30	34	5	21.05	105.25	105
8	35	38	4	21.05	84.20	84
9	39	43	1	21.05	21.05	
			4	18.70	74.80	
					95.85	96
10	44	48	5	18.70	93.50	94
11	49	53	5	18.70	93.50	94
12	54	58	5	18.70	93.50	94
13	59	62	4	18.70	74.80	75

We might want to compare the numbers that were derived against the original plan.

Week	Weekly Quantity	Cumulative Weekly Quantity	Month	Monthly	Cumulative Monthly Quantity	Cumulative Variances
1	76	76				
2	95	171				
3	95	266				
4	95	361	Jan	380	380	− 19
5	103	464				
6	105	569				
7	105	674				
8	84	758	Feb	400	780	− 22
9	96	854				
10	94	948				
11	94	1042				
12	94	1136				
13	75	1211	Mar	430	1210	+ 1

From the above example, you can draw two conclusions.

1. The resultant quantities per week are not nice and smooth across time. (Correct, because neither are the workdays per month or the quantities per month smooth across time.)
2. The variances show a large amount of deviation between the two plans. (Correct, because month end dates and week end dates are not necessarily the same dates.)

The simplistic approach for the conversion of months to weeks is the "four-four-five" approach. Assume that every quarter has 13 weeks. Within the quarter, month one has four weeks, month two has four weeks, and month three has five weeks. The comparison of both approaches is illustrated below.

Week	Workday Approach	Four-Four-Five Approach
1	76	95
2	95	95
3	95	95
4	95	95
5	103	100
6	105	100
7	105	100
8	84	100
9	96	86
10	94	86
11	94	86
12	94	86
13	75	86

In a very general sense, the four-four-five approach provides about the same quantities per week and appears to be an acceptable alternative.

We have now converted from monthly to weekly planning buckets. Now we must convert these planned weekly quantities to planned order quantities. Note that the above conversion could well have been a futile exercise if the minimum lot size for this item was, for example, 1000. It would have told us that we needed to receive an order for 1000 in week 10. We may well have been able to approximate the same thing on a monthly basis and save the whole bucket-size conversion calculation.

Let's assume a lot size, for the example, of a quantity of 75. Remember that the date (week number) is the time that the quantity is received from production, not the date that the shop order is released to production. Also, let us further constrain our example by saying that only the lot size or multiples of the lot size can be produced. Therefore, if 76 are required, and the lot size is 75, then 150 must be produced.

Our calculations to derive planned orders from the workday conversion might look like the following. (Note that the remaining weekly quantity from any period is applied to the order receipt in the next period.)

Week	Planned Weekly Quantity	Planned Order Receipt Quantity	Remaining Weekly Quantity
1	76	150	74
2	95	75	54
3	95	75	34
4	95	75	14
5	103	150	61
6	105	75	31
7	105	75	1
8	84	150	67
9	96	75	46
10	94	75	27
11	94	75	8
12	94	150	64
13	75	75	64
		Total	545
		Average	42

The planned orders from the four-four-five conversion would develop as follows.

Week	Planned Weekly Quantity	Planned Order Receipt Quantity	Remaining Weekly Quantity
1	95	150	55
2	95	75	35
3	95	75	15
4	95	150	70
5	100	75	45
6	100	75	20

(continued)

Week	Planned Weekly Quantity	Planned Order Receipt Quantity	Remaining Weekly Quantity
7	100	150	70
8	100	75	45
9	86	75	34
10	86	75	23
11	86	75	12
12	86	75	1
13	86	150	65
		Total	490
		Average	38

Some conclusions that might be drawn in this example from a comparison of the results of these two approaches are:

1. Both approaches planned four orders for quantities of 150.
2. Both approaches planned nine orders for quantities of 75.
3. The four-four-five approach has a lower average remaining inventory. (Note that this is not necessarily on-hand inventory, which is based on production minus gross demand.)
4. Either approach appears acceptable.

Now let's double the lot size and see what happens.

	Workday Approach			Four-Four-Five Approach		
Week	Planned Weekly Quantity	Planned Order Receipt Quantity	Remaining Weekly Quantity	Planned Weekly Quantity	Planned Order Receipt Quantity	Remaining Weekly Quantity
1	76	150	74	95	150	55
2	95	150	129	95	150	110
3	95		34	95		15
4	95	150	89	95	150	70
5	103	150	136	100	150	120
6	105		31	100		20
7	105	150	76	100	150	70
8	84	150	142	100	150	120
9	96		46	86		34

(continued)

	Workday Approach			Four-Four-Five Approach		
Week	Planned Weekly Quantity	Planned Order Receipt Quantity	Remaining Weekly Quantity	Planned Weekly Quantity	Planned Order Receipt Quantity	Remaining Weekly Quantity
10	94	150	102	86	150	98
11	94		8	86		12
12	94	150	64	86	150	76
13	75	150	139	86	150	140
		Total	1070			940
		Average	82			72

If we roughly halve the original lot size of 75 to 35, we obtain the following results.

	Workday Approach			Four-Four-Five Approach		
Week	Planned Weekly Quantity	Planned Order Receipt Quantity	Remaining Weekly Quantity	Planned Weekly Quantity	Planned Order Receipt Quantity	Remaining Weekly Quantity
1	76	105	29	95	105	10
2	95	70	4	95	105	20
3	95	105	14	95	105	30
4	95	105	24	95	70	5
5	103	105	26	100	105	10
6	105	105	26	100	105	15
7	105	105	26	100	105	20
8	84	70	12	100	105	25
9	96	105	21	86	70	9
10	94	105	32	86	105	28
11	94	70	8	86	70	12
12	94	105	19	86	105	31
13	75	70	14	86	70	15
		Total	255			230
		Average	20			18

You have probably concluded by now that either approach is acceptable. You should have also noticed that:

1. The larger the lot size, the larger the average remaining weekly quantity.
2. The four-four-five approach has a lower average remaining weekly quantity than the workday approach.

If you are agreeing with the logic at this point and not asking some other questions, then you have been led into a trap. Many companies find themselves in this same trap and never understand how it happened.

In the workday approach, we needed 380 items for January. The month had 20 workdays, so this translated to 19 items per day. Week one had four days, so we calculated that 76 items were required for that week. Now we are proposing to make 105 items instead of 76. In week two we required 95 items, be we're only going to produce 70.

The trap was the initial constraint that the lot size or a multiple of that quantity must be used. We could have set the lot size at 70 as a minimum and had the maximum be any quantity more than 70, such as 76, or 95, or 103. If we had done this, there never would have been any remaining weekly quantity with either of the two approaches. The real difference between the two approaches is shown below.

Week	Days Per Week	Workday Approach		Four-Four-Five Approach	
		Planned Quantity	Daily Rate	Planned Quantity	Daily Rate
1	4	76	19	95	24
2	5	95	19	95	19
3	5	95	19	95	19
4	5	95	19	95	19
5	5	103	21	100	20
6	5	105	21	100	20
7	5	105	21	100	20
8	4	84	21	100	25
9	5	96	19	86	17
10	5	94	19	86	17
11	5	94	19	86	17
12	5	94	19	86	17
13	4	75	19	86	22

There is less stability in the daily rate of the four-four-five approach than the workday approach. Recognize that the need for stability decreases with an increase in the quantiity of the lot size. Conversely, the greater the concern with a stable daily rate, the closer the lot size approaches a quantity of one.

The message in this section is that new users of MPSP should not just assume that the lot sizes that they have used for 20 years are necessarily adequate or correct. An in-depth analysis of the lot sizes should be performed to determine why they exist and what will be the results if they are used. Also, since lot sizes are normally based on machine set-up times, the first implementation step should be to reduce those set-up times, and therefore, the lot size quantity. Once this is understood, then the proper technique for bucket conversion can be selected.

POSSIBLE MSP DISPLAYS

Various displays are necessary to manage the master schedule for an item. One format that is very useful is shown below.

Item 614   Lot Size: 600   On-Hand Quantity: 800

Date	Planned Order Number	Quantity	Item Production Plan	Blended Gross Demand	Projected Inventory
03/02			384	400	400
03/09			330	400	0
03/16	O123	600	402	400	200
03/23	O126	600	227	400	400
03/30			350	400	0
04/06	O139	600	235	400	200
04/13	O146	600	340	400	400
04/20			317	400	0
04/20	Demand Time Fence				
04/27	F152	600	445	400	200
05/04	F160	600	284	400	400
05/04	CMLT				
05/11			366	400	0
05/18	P172	600	320	400	200
05/25	P181	600	330	400	400

The "O," the "F," and the "P" attached to the planned order number indicates an open order (released to the shop), a firm planned order, (the planned quantity is not to be recalculated) and a planned order (the system is allowed to recalculate the quantity in the next planning cycle), respectively.

A cumulative material lead time (CMLT) is established to indicate how far into the future planned orders should be frozen. It indicates that if a quantity of 600 is to be built for period 05/04, then the material/parts should be ordered now. Any planned orders within the CMLT should generate a message to the master scheduler so that he or she can make the decision to firm the order or not. The master scheduler could also change the order quantity, which would also cause the order to be firmed.

The demand time fence is the control that tells the system to start creating orders to build the product. Note that if order quantities are changed at this time, the previously ordered material/parts will probably be short or in excess.

Another useful display is one to analyze demand for an item, as shown below.

Item 918

Date	Forecast Quantity	Booked Quantity	Blended Gross Demand
03/02	60	60	60
03/09	70	70	70
03/16	80	75	75
03/23	90	80	80
03/30	100	90	90
03/30		Demand time fence	
04/06	120	100	120
04/13	160	120	160
04/20	100	90	100
04/20		CMLT	
04/27	80	60	80
05/04	70	40	70
05/11	60	20	60
05/18	60	10	60
05/25	60	0	60

Note that the blend algorithm in the above display uses the greater of forecast or booked sales by period, except within the demand item fence, when only booked sales are used. This could mean that in period 04/13, for example, parts would be ordered for 160 items and 120 might be all that are actually sold. This display, however, provides the master scheduler with the ability to view trends in demand and make adjustments in the master schedule accordingly.

An available-to-promise (ATP) display is an extremely useful screen for the order entry department. When a customer phones an order in, it enables the clerk to quote a shipping date with a reasonable degree of accuracy. Note that to maintain accuracy, this display has to be updated every time an order is booked.

Item: 224   Lot Size: 200   On-Hand Quantity: 40

Date	Blended Gross Demand	Production Orders	Booked Orders Per Period	Cumulative Booked Orders	Projected Ending Inventory	Next Production Period Required Inventory	ATP
03/02	60	200	60				
03/09	70		70				
03/16	75		75	205	35	0	35
03/23	80	200	80				
03/30	90		90	170	65	0	65
04/06	120	200	100	100	165	70	95
04/13	160	200	120				
04/20	100		90				
04/27	80		60	270	95	0	95
05/04	70	200	40				
05/11	60		20				
05/18	60		10	70	225	0	225
05/25	60	200	0	0	425	0	425

The production orders were calculated from item production plans. The blended gross demand has been illustrated as comparison data to the master scheduler. The projected ending inventory is the production orders plus any previous inventory balance minus the cumulative booked orders. The quantity in "Next Production Period Required Inventory" is the total booked orders minus the production orders. The ATP is the "Projected Ending Inventory" minus the "Next Production Period Required Inventory."

Note that not all of the columns in the above example are illustrated in the normal ATP display. The results of the calculations are sometimes illustrated as shown below.

Item: 224   Lot Size: 200   On-Hand Quantity: 40

Date	Production Orders	Booked Orders	ATP
03/02	200	60	0
03/09		70	0
03/16		75	0
03/23	200	80	0

(continued)

Item: 224   Lot Size: 200   On-Hand Quantity: 40 (continued)

Date	Production Orders	Booked Orders	ATP
03/30		90	0
03/30	Demand time fence		
04/06	200	100	95
04/13	200	120	95
04/20		90	95
04/20	CMLT		
04/27		60	95
05/04	200	40	225
05/11		20	225
05/18		10	225
05/25	200	0	425

Note that within the demand time fence, the ATP is zero. Many companies would actually extend this to the CMLT in order to better manage material. The decision is a trade off. Do you really want a frozen zone that totally controls material or do you want some flexibility (as planning to gross demand between the CMLT and the demand time fence) to pick up that extra sale?

Note that the planned orders are also tested via rough-cut capacity planning, which is discussed in the next section.

PART FIVE

RESOURCE PLANNING

CHAPTER NINE

BUILDING AN ITEM RESOURCE PROFILE

SOME BASIC DEFINITIONS

The general category of resource planning is often thought of as consisting of two subfunctions: resource requirements planning and rough-cut capacity planning.

Resource requirements planning (RRP) is normally performed at a product family level using family resource profiles. These profiles consist of item resource profiles structured by some mix percentage relationship. The intent of RRP is to provide top management with data regarding the impact of the production plan on the total plant(s). As such, the planning bucket size is usually large (such as a month or a quarter) and the horizon is usually long (such as three to five years). The types of data that are of concern at this planning level may be:

Total direct labor hours required
Total machine hours required (by work center)
Total costs (labor, machine, and overhead)

While RRP applies to master production planning at a family level, rough-cut capacity planning (RCCP) applies to master schedule planning at an item level. The profiles are item profiles. They are the same item profiles that were used to construct the family profiles in RRP. The intent of RCCP is to provide management with the data regarding the impact of lot-sized master schedule orders on selected critical or bottleneck work centers. As such, the planning period is shorter than in RRP, normally a day, week, or month, and the horizon is normally shorter, such as six to 18 months. The types of data that are of concern at this planning level may be:

Labor hours required
Machine hours required

Note that the designated resource utilized to create a profile may be almost anything, such as required square feet of floor space. This type of resource would normally be entered manually into the system as a requirement.

A SIMPLE ITEM PROFILE

Imagine that two items are to be planned, an "A" and a "B." Each of the two items can be completely fabricated using one routing that flows through three work centers. The routings (in a simplistic version) are shown below.

Item A

Operation Number	Work Center	Time in Days	Description
010	101	2.0	Do thing A
020	406	1.0	Do thing B
030	101	2.0	Do thing C
040	602	4.0	Do thing D
050	101	2.0	Do thing E
060	406	1.0	Do thing F
		Total 12.0	

Item B

Operation Number	Work Center	Time in Days	Description
010	406	1.0	Do thing G
020	602	5.0	Do thing H
030	101	2.0	Do thing I
040	101	3.0	Do thing J
050	602	4.0	Do thing K
060	406	1.0	Do thing L
		Total 16.0	

It takes 12 days to produce an A and 16 days to produce a B.

We need to build an item resource profile. This is a description of how much resource is required to produce one of an item, and when. An easy way to illustrate the calculations for profile construction is shown below.

Item A

Operation Number	Operation Time	Cumulative Time	Cumulative Minus Total (Offset)	Applied to Work Center		
				101	406	602
010	2.0	2.0	−10.0	2.0		
020	1.0	3.0	−9.0		1.0	
030	2.0	5.0	−7.0	2.0		
040	4.0	9.0	−3.0			4.0
050	2.0	11.0	−1.0	2.0		
060	1.0	12.0	−0.0		1.0	

Item B

Operation Number	Operation Time	Cumulative Time	Cumulative Minus Total (Offset)	Applied to Work Center		
				101	406	602
010	1.0	1.0	−15.0		1.0	
020	5.0	6.0	−10.0			5.0
030	2.0	8.0	−8.0	2.0		
040	3.0	11.0	−5.0	3.0		
050	4.0	15.0	−1.0			4.0
060	1.0	16.0	−0.0		1.0	

The item profiles may now be summarized as in the following example.

Item	Offset	Required Resource	Work Center
A	− 0.0	1.0	406
A	− 1.0	2.0	101
A	− 3.0	4.0	602
A	− 7.0	2.0	101
A	− 9.0	1.0	406
A	− 10.0	2.0	101
B	− 0.0	1.0	406
B	− 1.0	4.0	602
B	− 5.0	3.0	101
B	− 8.0	2.0	101
B	− 10.0	5.0	602
B	− 15.0	1.0	406

We have now calculated the resource profile records to make one of each of these two items. There are some additional considerations to the creation of resource profiles.

Some companies elect not to calculate the profiles as we have just described. It may be that their routings are not accurate, or they may not even have routings. These companies would manually enter the above profile records.

Some companies do not wish to calculate a profile based on every available work center. They wish to flag only those work centers that are considered to be critical. This rational is frequently applied in rough-cut capacity planning.

In the above example, we considered a resource called time. The general category can be subdivided into:

Input queue time
Set-up time
Run time
Output queue time
Move time

The set-up and run times may also be viewed as machine and/or direct labor requirements. These in turn can be calculated in terms of hours or costs to which work center overheads can be applied.

THE COMPOSITE ITEM PROFILE

Assume that you wish to construct an item resource profile for product "X." The product structure for an X is shown in Figure 9.1. The indented bill of material for product X is shown below.

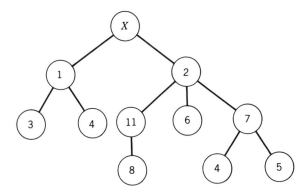

FIGURE 9.1 Product structure for an X.

Item Identification	Quantity Per	Lead Time	Item Type
X	1	5	Manufacture
— 1	2	15	Manufacture
— — 3	1	10	Purchase
— — 4	1	10	Purchase
— 2	3	20	Manufacture
— — 11	1	10	Manufacture
— — — 8	1	10	Purchase
— — 6	2	10	Purchase
— — 7	2	20	Manufacture
— — — 4	1	10	Purchase
— — — 5	1	10	Purchase

Figure 9.2 is another way to illustrate the lead time offsets required to produce an X. You can see that the total time required (the cumulative material lead time or CMLT) is 55 days. However, since we are not considering purchase components as consuming our work center resources, the actual manufacturing process starts with item 7, for a total of 45 required days.

Each component in product structure X will have an item profile. Product X will also have an item profile, but since the profile for product X is a composite of the components that make up an X, it is often referred to as a composite item profile. Note that any item, as for example item 2, that is composed of lower level profiles is also a composite profile.

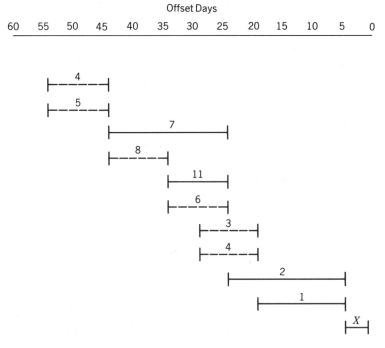

FIGURE 9.2   Lead time offsets of product X. (Dashed lines represent purchasing lead times.)

When changes are made to an item profile (for example, due to product structure or routing changes) a profile "where used" should be performed, and all of the composite profiles that utilized the item profile should be flagged for recalculation.

The composite profile calculation is a two direction process. First, explode the bill of material down through the structure levels to determine those profiles that need recalculation. Second, from the lowest level moving up through the structure, recalculate the flagged profiles. If we assume that all levels are recalculated in our example for product X, we might generate the following resource profile records for components 7 and 11.

Item	Offset	Required Resource	Work Center
7	− 0	4	220
7	− 4	2	101
7	− 6	2	290
7	− 8	3	150
7	− 11	2	101
7	− 13	5	220
7	− 18	2	101
11	− 0	5	101
11	− 5	5	290

Another way to view these profile records is shown in the data on pages 144 and 145, which illustrate the cumulative resource requirement by work center.

The cumulative values have been calculated from the largest offset to the smallest.

We now have some definition of a required resource for two items. These are true item resource profiles since they are not composed of any lower product structure level profiles.

The next level up in our structure was item 2. It is composed of the resources required in its own routing, plus the profiles for items 7 and 11.

Let us assume that some very large queues exist in the assembly of an item 2. If we can assume that the resource we have been measuring is direct labor, then items 7 and 11 had no queues since the required resource consumed the available time. Now to assemble an item 2 from an item 7 and an item 11, 50% of our time is consumed in a wait mode (sitting in queues), and the remaining 50% applies to direct labor. Our cumulative data calculation might look like that on page 146 for the routing of item 2.

That data is not yet a profile of item 2 since it does not reflect items 7 and 11, which must be added to develop the composite item profile. First the cumulatives of items 7 and 11 must be added together, since they are a prerequisite to the start of the item 2 routing (see page 147).

When the item 2 prerequisite cumulatives are combined with the item 2 routing cumulatives, we obtain the picture on pages 148 and 149.

We have now created a composite resource profile for item 2.

A similar approach would be used to calculate the routing item profiles for item 1 and item X. The profile for item 1 would be added to the item 2 profile. The item X (our end item) routing profile would be extended to provide the total composite product X profile.

Note that a profile will exist for every item in every level of the product

Item 7

Work Center

Offset	101		150		220		290	
	Quantity	Cumulative	Quantity	Cumulative	Quantity	Cumulative	Quantity	Cumulative
-0	—	6	—	3	4	9	—	2
-1	—	6	—	3	—	5	—	2
-2	—	6	—	3	—	5	—	2
-3	—	6	—	3	—	5	—	2
-4	2	6	—	3	—	5	—	2
-5	—	4	—	3	—	5	—	2
-6	—	4	—	3	—	5	2	2
-7	—	4	—	3	—	5	—	0
-8	—	4	3	3	—	5	—	0
-9	—	4	—	0	—	5	—	0
-10	—	4	—	0	—	5	—	0
-11	2	4	—	0	—	5	—	0
-12	—	2	—	0	—	5	—	0
-13	—	2	—	0	5	5	—	0
-14	—	2	—	0	—	0	—	0
-15	—	2	—	0	—	0	—	0
-16	—	2	—	0	—	0	—	0
-17	—	2	—	0	—	0	—	0
-18	2	2	—	0	—	0	—	0

Item 11

Work Center

Offset	101 Quantity	101 Cumulative	150 Quantity	150 Cumulative	220 Quantity	220 Cumulative	290 Quantity	290 Cumulative
—0	5	5	—	0	—	0	—	5
—1	—	0	—	0	—	0	—	5
—2	—	0	—	0	—	0	—	5
—3	—	0	—	0	—	0	—	5
—4	—	0	—	0	—	0	—	5
—5	—	0	—	0	—	0	5	5

Item 2

Work Center

Offset	101 Quantity	101 Cumulative	150 Quantity	150 Cumulative	220 Quantity	220 Cumulative	290 Quantity	290 Cumulative
−0	2	2	—	3	—	2	—	3
−1	—	0	—	3	—	2	—	3
−2	—	0	—	3	—	2	—	3
−3	—	0	—	3	—	2	—	3
−4	—	0	3	3	—	2	—	3
−5	—	0	—	0	—	2	—	3
−6	—	0	—	0	—	2	—	3
−7	—	0	—	0	—	2	—	3
−8	—	0	—	0	—	2	—	3
−9	—	0	—	0	—	2	—	3
−10	—	0	—	0	2	2	—	3
−11	—	0	—	0	—	0	—	3
−12	—	0	—	0	—	0	—	3
−13	—	0	—	0	—	0	—	3
−14	—	0	—	0	—	0	3	3

Item 2 Prerequisite Work Center Cumulatives

Work Center

Offset	101			150			220			290		
	Item 7	Item 11	Total	Item 7	Item 11	Total	Item 7	Item 11	Total	Item 7	Item 11	Total
-0	6	5	11	3	0	3	9	0	9	2	5	7
-1	6	0	6	3	0	3	5	0	5	2	5	7
-2	6	0	6	3	0	3	5	0	5	2	5	7
-3	6	0	6	3	0	3	5	0	5	2	5	7
-4	6	0	6	3	0	3	5	0	5	2	5	7
-5	4	0	4	3	0	3	5	0	5	2	5	7
-6	4	0	4	3	0	3	5	0	5	2	0	2
-7	4	0	4	3	0	3	5	0	5	0	0	0
-8	4	0	4	3	0	3	5	0	5	0	0	0
-9	4	0	4	0	0	0	5	0	5	0	0	0
-10	4	0	4	0	0	0	5	0	5	0	0	0
-11	4	0	4	0	0	0	5	0	5	0	0	0
-12	2	0	2	0	0	0	5	0	5	0	0	0
-13	2	0	2	0	0	0	5	0	5	0	0	0
-14	2	0	2	0	0	0	0	0	0	0	0	0
-15	2	0	2	0	0	0	0	0	0	0	0	0
-16	2	0	2	0	0	0	0	0	0	0	0	0
-17	2	0	2	0	0	0	0	0	0	0	0	0
-18	2	0	2	0	0	0	0	0	0	0	0	0

Item 2 Composite Profile

Work Center

Total Item 2 Offset	101			150			220			290		
	Item 2 Cum.	Item 7/11 Cum.	Total Cum.	Item 2 Cum.	Item 7/11 Cum.	Total Cum.	Item 2 Cum.	Item 7/11 Cum.	Total Cum.	Item 2 Cum.	Item 7/11 Cum.	Total Cum.
−0	2	11	13	3	3	6	2	9	11	3	7	10
−1	0	11	11	3	3	6	2	9	11	3	7	10
−2	0	11	11	3	3	6	2	9	11	3	7	10
−3	0	11	11	3	3	6	2	9	11	3	7	10
−4	0	11	11	3	3	6	2	9	11	3	7	10
−5	0	11	11	0	3	3	2	9	11	3	7	10
−6	0	11	11	0	3	3	2	9	11	3	7	10
−7	0	11	11	0	3	3	2	9	11	3	7	10
−8	0	11	11	0	3	3	2	9	11	3	7	10
−9	0	11	11	0	3	3	2	9	11	3	7	10
−10	0	11	11	0	3	3	0	9	9	3	7	10
−11	0	11	11	0	3	3	0	9	9	3	7	10
−12	0	11	11	0	3	3	0	9	9	3	7	10
−13	0	11	11	0	3	3	0	9	9	3	7	10
−14	0	11	11	0	3	3	0	9	9	3	7	10
−15	0	11	11	0	3	3	0	9	9	0	7	7

	-16	-17	-18	-19	-20	-21	-22	-23	-24	-25	-26	-27	-28	-29	-30	-31	-32	-33	-34	-35	-36	-37	-38
	1	1	1	1	1	1	1	1	1	1	1	2	0	0	0	0	0	0	0	0	0	0	0
	1	1	1	1	1	1	1	1	1	1	1	2	0	0	0	0	0	0	0	0	0	0	0
	0	0	0	0	0	0	0	0	0	0	0	0	0	0	0	0	0	0	0	0	0	0	0
	9	9	9	9	9	5	5	5	5	5	5	5	5	5	5	5	5	0	0	0	0	0	0
	9	9	9	9	9	5	5	5	5	5	5	5	5	5	5	5	5	0	0	0	0	0	0
	0	0	0	0	0	0	0	0	0	0	0	0	0	0	0	0	0	0	0	0	0	0	0
	3	3	3	3	3	3	3	3	3	3	3	3	3	0	0	0	0	0	0	0	0	0	0
	3	3	3	3	3	3	3	3	3	3	3	3	3	0	0	0	0	0	0	0	0	0	0
	0	0	0	0	0	0	0	0	0	0	0	0	0	0	0	0	0	0	0	0	0	0	0
	11	11	11	11	11	6	6	6	6	4	4	4	4	4	4	4	2	2	2	2	2	2	2
	11	11	11	11	11	6	6	6	6	4	4	4	4	4	4	4	2	2	2	2	2	2	2
	0	0	0	0	0	0	0	0	0	0	0	0	0	0	0	0	0	0	0	0	0	0	0

structure. Item 11 is at the second level in the product X bill of material. In another product, item 11 may be at the same or any other level. There is no need to recalculate the item 11 profile. Once it has been calculated and stored, it can be retrieved whenever it is encountered in any end item (or planned item) structure.

Although we now have composite profiles, we probably have too much detail. We have been offseting in terms of days. We need these quantities grouped into the necessary planning period size, which might be a month in MPP, or a week in MSP.

If our item 2 had been our final planning item (instead of product X) and we assume five days per week with four weeks per month, we can derive the following data.

	Offset in			Work Center 101 Cumulative Requirements by	
Days	Weeks	Months	Day	Week	Month
−0	−0	−0	13	13	13
−1			11		
−2			11		
−3			11		
−4			11		
−5	−1		11	11	
−6			11		
−7			11		
−8			11		
−9			11		
−10	−2		11	11	
−11			11		
−12			11		
−13			11		
−14			11		

Offset in			Work Center 101 Cumulative Requirements by		
Days	Weeks	Months	Day	Week	Month
− 15	− 3		11	11	
− 16			11		
− 17			11		
− 18			11		
− 19			11		
− 20	− 4	− 1	11	11	11
− 21			6		
− 22			6		
− 23			6		
− 24			6		
− 25	− 5		4	4	
− 26			4		
− 27			4		
− 28			4		
− 29			4		
− 30	− 6		4	4	
− 31			4		
− 32			2		
− 33			2		
− 34			2		
− 35	− 7		2	2	
− 36			2		
− 37			2		
− 38			2		

At this point, you should be starting to understand why we have been dealing with cumulative values. It is now very easy to figure the resource profile by any planning bucket size that we might select. For example, if we wish to know how much work center 101 direct labor is required by weekly planning bucket, our calculations will be as shown below.

Offset Week	Cumulative Amount	Minus Previous Period	Required Resource Quantity
−0	13	11	2
−1	11	11	0
−3	11	11	0
−4	11	4	7
−5	4	4	0
−6	4	2	2
−7	2	0	2
		Total	13

Or, if we were to perform the calculation by month, we would derive the following.

Offset Month	Cumulative Amount	Minus Previous Period	Required Resource Quantity
−0	13	11	2
−1	11	0	11
		Total	13

The next section discusses how the composite item profiles can be structured into families.

CHAPTER TEN

BUILDING A FAMILY RESOURCE PROFILE

ITEM PROFILE MIX PERCENTAGES IN THE FAMILY

Consider the following situation. We have decided to structure a product family with four items. The production plan is as shown below.

Product Family Production Plan

Period	Total Plan	Item 1	Item 2	Item 3	Item 4
1	454	30	384	40	0
2	460	80	330	40	10
3	552	100	402	30	20
4	437	160	227	20	30
5	460	60	350	10	40
6	345	60	235	0	50
7	460	60	340	0	60
8	437	50	317	0	70
9	575	50	445	0	80
10	414	50	284	0	80
11	506	60	366	0	80
12	460	60	320	0	80
Totals	5560	820	4000	140	600

The mix percentages of these production plans are illustrated below.

Period	Item 1	Item 2	Item 3	Item 4
1	0.066	0.846	0.088	0
2	0.174	0.717	0.087	0.022
3	0.181	0.728	0.054	0.036
4	0.366	0.519	0.046	0.069
5	0.130	0.761	0.022	0.087
6	0.174	0.681	0	0.145
7	0.130	0.739	0	0.130
8	0.114	0.725	0	0.160
9	0.087	0.774	0	0.139
10	0.121	0.686	0	0.193
11	0.119	0.723	0	0.158
12	0.130	0.696	0	0.174
Horizon percentage	0.147	0.719	0.025	0.108

There are three ways to address the mix percentages of item resource profiles in a family.

The simplest approach is to enter a manually calculated or a "gut-feel" percentage that applies across all periods. In this example, these numbers might be:

Item	Percentage
1	15
2	70
3	3
4	12

Note that this approach will apply 12% of the resource profile of item 4 to period one (when none is needed) and 3% of the resource profile of item 3 to periods six through 12, when again, none is needed.

A second approach is to calculate the horizon percentages and apply those as:

Item	Percentage
1	15
2	72
3	2
4	11

This approach is slightly better than the simple approach, although not much better if accuracy is desired. It is plagued with the same problems. Some companies will modify this approach with start/stop dates on the percentages based on major product mix changes. For example, period one may have one set of percentages. Periods two through five may have a second set of percentages (item 3 is phasing out and item 4 is starting up). Periods six through 12 have a third set of percentages. Obviously whether this approach is good or bad is dependent on the degree of accuracy that is desired by the user.

The third approach is to use the period mix percentages. If you elect this approach, then you are no longer constrained by specific product family construction criteria (as all items in a family should consume about the same amount of the same resources).

Using this approach, you can construct your product families based on common costs, or common raw materials, or anything else, and you will still apply a realistic percentage of the resources that are consumed by the items in the period.

The disadvantage to this third approach is that the percentages will constantly change. It is January. You calculate the mix percentages for all items in all families. As January passes, things happen that were not planned. Demand patterns change. Production is over or under. A cycle count results in adjustments to your inventory records. Eventually it is February, and you have to recalculate all of your mix percentages. If you need the accuracy, this is a good approach, but it is expensive in computer processing time.

WHAT IS A FAMILY PROFILE?

An item resource profile is a description of what resources are required to produce one of the product. If the production process or the product structure (bill of material) does not change, the item profile does not change. In theory, our product item profile could be used forever.

But now we have something called a family resource profile. The name is similar, but usually that is where the similarity stops.

If we had a product family consisting of item 1 and item 2, and item 1 was *always* 75% and item 2 was *always* 25%, the concept of a family profile would be similar to an item profile. It would not really matter which of the three techniques were used to define the mix relationship of the items in the family. It is always 75% and 25%.

The family resource profile represents the resources required to build one (granted, this is a theoretical "one") of the family. We can now extend the quantity of resources by the production plan quantities as they vary from period to period.

However, there is only one situation that would allow for the above product family example to exist. The sales trends for items 1 and 2 would have to be identical. Also, the inventory levels would have to be such so that when net demands were calculated, the 75%–25% relationship was maintained.

A reasonable probability exists that not many product families of this type will exist. More often than not, item inventories will vary. Mix percentages of items in the family will vary by period. Therefore, the family resource profile will exist for a very short time, often only a single period.

Another modification is not to use mix percentages to build and maintain family resource profiles, but rather to extend item profiles by the item quantities in the family by period. This is usually practical only if a computer is being used to perform the calculations.

Let's continue with our previous example for mix percentages of four items in a family. Let's also assume that you have item resource profiles for each of the four items. Assume that the resource is direct labor for Work Center 603. The requirements for this resource are shown below, by item.

Offset Month	Item 1	Item 2	Item 3	Item 4
−0	10	40	80	5
−1	5	5	0	5
−2	20	2	0	5
−3	0	1	0	30

This means, for item 1 for example, it takes three months to make an item 1. The first month takes 20 hours of resources, the second month takes five hours, and the third (when the item 1 is complete) takes 10 hours.

We need to extend each item's profile in the periods where items consume resources. Let's start in the last period (of the horizon) and work backward to now. The production plan of our example for period 12 was:

Item	Planned Quantity
1	60
2	320
3	0
4	80
Total	460

The calculation for period 12 is:

	Item 1 Hours for		Item 2 Hours for		Item 3 Hours for		Item 4 Hours for		Total Resource
Period	1	60	1	320	1	0	1	80	Hours
12	10	600	40	12,800	80	0	5	400	13,800
11	5	300	5	1,600	0	0	5	400	2,300
10	20	1,200	2	640	0	0	5	400	2,240
9	0	0	1	320	0	0	30	2,400	2,720

The calculations for the remaining 11 periods are shown below.

Period 11

	Item 1 Hours for		Item 2 Hours for		Item 3 Hours for		Item 4 Hours for		Total Resource
Period	1	60	1	366	1	0	1	80	Hours
11	10	600	40	14,640	80	0	5	400	15,640
10	5	300	5	1,830	0	0	5	400	2,530
9	20	1,200	2	732	0	0	5	400	2,332
8	0	0	1	366	0	0	30	2,400	2,766

Period 10

	Item 1 Hours for		Item 2 Hours for		Item 3 Hours for		Item 4 Hours for		Total Resource
Period	1	50	1	284	1	0	1	80	Hours
10	10	500	40	11,360	80	0	5	400	12,260
9	5	250	5	1,420	0	0	5	400	2,070
8	20	1,000	2	568	0	0	5	400	1,968
7	0	0	1	284	0	0	30	2,400	2,684

Period 9

Period	Item 1 Hours for		Item 2 Hours for		Item 3 Hours for		Item 4 Hours for		Total Resource Hours
	1	60	1	320	1	0	1	80	
9	10	500	40	17,800	80	0	5	400	18,700
8	5	250	5	2,225	0	0	5	400	2,875
7	20	1,000	2	890	0	0	5	400	1,290
6	0	0	1	445	0	0	30	2,400	2,845

Period 8

Period	Item 1 Hours for		Item 2 Hours for		Item 3 Hours for		Item 4 Hours for		Total Resource Hours
	1	50	1	317	1	0	1	70	
8	10	500	40	12,680	80	0	5	350	13,530
7	5	250	5	1,585	0	0	5	350	2,185
6	20	1,000	2	634	0	0	5	350	1,984
5	0	0	1	317	0	0	30	2,100	2,417

Period 7

Period	Item 1 Hours for		Item 2 Hours for		Item 3 Hours for		Item 4 Hours for		Total Resource Hours
	1	60	1	340	1	0	1	60	
7	10	600	40	13,600	80	0	5	300	14,500
6	5	300	5	1,700	0	0	5	300	2,300
5	20	1,200	2	680	0	0	5	300	2,180
4	0	0	1	340	0	0	30	1,800	2,140

Period 6

Period	Item 1 Hours for		Item 2 Hours for		Item 3 Hours for		Item 4 Hours for		Total Resource Hours
	1	60	1	235	1	0	1	50	
6	10	600	40	9,400	80	0	5	250	10,250
5	5	300	5	1,175	0	0	5	250	1,725
4	20	1,200	2	470	0	0	5	250	1,920
3	0	0	1	235	0	0	30	1,500	1,735

Period 5

Period	Item 1 Hours for		Item 2 Hours for		Item 3 Hours for		Item 4 Hours for		Total Resource Hours
	1	60	1	350	1	10	1	40	
5	10	600	40	14,000	80	800	5	200	15,600
4	5	300	5	1,750	0	0	5	200	2,250
3	20	1,200	2	700	0	0	5	200	2,100
2	0	0	1	350	0	0	30	1,200	1,550

Period 4

Period	Item 1 Hours for		Item 2 Hours for		Item 3 Hours for		Item 4 Hours for		Total Resource Hours
	1	60	1	227	1	20	1	30	
4	10	1,600	40	9,080	80	1,600	5	150	12,430
3	5	800	5	1,135	0	0	5	150	2,085
2	20	3,200	2	454	0	0	5	150	3,804
1	0	0	1	227	0	0	30	900	1,127

Period 3

	Item 1 Hours for		Item 2 Hours for		Item 3 Hours for		Item 4 Hours for		Total Resource
Period	1	100	1	402	1	30	1	20	Hours
3	10	1,000	40	16,080	80	2,400	5	100	19,500
2	5	500	5	2,010	0	0	5	100	2,610
1	20	2,000	2	804	0	0	5	100	2,904
0	0	0	1	402	0	0	30	600	1,002

Period 2

	Item 1 Hours for		Item 2 Hours for		Item 3 Hours for		Item 4 Hours for		Total Resource
Period	1	80	1	330	1	40	1	10	Hours
2	10	800	40	13,200	80	3,200	5	50	17,250
1	5	400	5	1,650	0	0	5	50	2,100
0	20	1,600	2	660	0	0	5	50	2,310
−1	0	0	1	330	0	0	30	300	630

Period 1

	Item 1 Hours for		Item 2 Hours for		Item 3 Hours for		Item 4 Hours for		Total Resource
Period	1	30	1	384	1	40	1	0	Hours
1	10	300	40	15,360	80	3,200	5	0	18,860
0	5	150	5	1,920	0	0	5	0	2,070
−1	20	600	2	768	0	0	5	0	1,368
−2	0	0	1	384	0	0	30	0	384

The summary of the required direct labor for Work Center 603 to meet the production plan for this specific product family is shown on the next page.

Calculation Period

Planning Period	1	2	3	4	5	6	7	8	9	10	11	12	Total
−2	384												384
−1	1368	630											1,998
0	2070	2310	1002										5,382
1	18860	2100	2904	1127									24,991
2		17250	2610	3804	1550								25,214
3			19580	2085	2100	1735							25,500
4				12430	2250	1920	2140						18,740
5					15600	1725	2180	2417					21,922
6						10250	2300	1984	2845				17,379
7							14500	2185	1290	2684			20,659
8								13530	2875	1968	2766		21,139
9									18700	2070	2332	2720	25,822
10										12260	2530	2240	17,030
11											15640	2300	17,940
12												13800	13,800

The data in periods 0, -1, and -2 are not too useful, since they do not reflect the production in those past periods. Also, these are past periods in which the effective utilization of the resources should already have been managed. Likewise, the data in periods 10, 11, and 12 are incomplete, since we have a four-month overlap and do not know the plan for periods 13, 14, and 15.

Let's round and summarize the remaining data in the total column in terms of thousands of hours.

					Period						
	1	2	3	4	5	6	7	8	9	Total	Average
Total	25.0	25.2	25.5	18.7	21.9	17.4	20.7	21.1	25.8	201.3	22.4

The conclusions that might be drawn from this exercise are:

1. The process requires extensive arithmetic calculations. (This was only direct labor for one work center.)
2. Mix percentages of items in the family were not used to derive the family resource requirements.
3. Had horizon mix percentages been used (either manually entered or calculated), they would not have detected the severe dips in periods 4 and 6.
4. Had a horizon mix percentage that was an average been used, the peaks in periods 1, 2, 3, and 9 would have been missed, and the production plan would probably not have been satisfied.

You have now reviewed some approaches to converting item profiles to family plan requirements. For MPP resource requirements planning, all family plans must be added together to derive the total production plan requirements. The results should be easily displayed as numerical values, or graphically as a bar chart, by period. The bar chart is useful because a second bar per period can be added to illustrate the anticipated available capacity for the period (to compare with what is required).

If the item resource profiles are used for rough-cut capacity planning in master schedule planning, the item profiles would have been extended by the planned order quantities and displayed in a manner similar to that employed in master production planning.

Remember that the prime function of resource planning is to create and maintain item resource profiles. How the item profile is handled at a family level depends upon your need for accurate or generalized data.

SUMMARY

A lot of material has been covered in this text. Examples have been used at times to illustrate where some techniques work better than others. The reader is encouraged to build test examples to validate desired techniques prior to building or buying an MPSP system. What works well for Company A may not work at all for Company B.

As you can tell by scanning the Table of Contents, the emphasis of this book has been on the techniques of MPSP as opposed to presenting one MPSP system and describing how you should use it. To my knowledge, no single MPSP software system in existence today utilizes all of the techniques described in this text.

My closing comment is—"look before you leap." MPSP is not like MRP, where the concepts are clearly understood by everyone. With MPSP, ten companies will give ten different descriptions of what MPSP should do. However, they really all hope to accomplish the same objectives. The differences exist in terminology and selected techniques. The terminology really doesn't matter once you learn the multiple meanings for a word or phrase. The selected techniques do matter. They identify how you will manage your business. Get MPSP education, select the right operational techniques for your business, and you will be on the way to installing your most important planning system.

APPENDIX I

WHERE MPSP FITS WITHIN THE FUNCTIONS OF A TYPICAL INDUSTRIAL SECTOR COMPANY

INTRODUCTION

Many companies will often structure functional applications in the same manner that they structure the company's organization. MPSP, however, is one of those applications that may easily cross organizational boundaries. Sometimes it is difficult to ascertain where MPSP best fits functionally in a typical industrial sector company. Each company will vary functional structure relationships according to how important they view their functions in relation to MPSP.

In order to provide you with the relationship of MPSP to supporting MPSP application areas, the appendix provides an application grouping based on organization structure. It illustrates the applications that usually fit within specific organizational functional areas. These in turn are categorized within major business areas. Note that this analysis is for a typical industrial sector company and will not totally apply to any one particular company.

Master production schedule planning has been categorized as section, "A. Master Production Schedule Planning" under Section, "VIII Product Planning and Control." Although it is logical to classify applications in specific organizational groupings, these groupings sometimes tend to merge and blend as systems are designed to perform specific applications such as MPSP. As such, this book covers MPSP as well as some of the applications in related areas as,

"C. Capacity Planning" and "D. Plant Rate Planning".
The material has been structured into this format.

I.   Major business area
        A.   Functional area
                1.   Application

It is possible for an application to fit into more than one functional area. This text, however, has categorized applications into specific functional areas based on where they would have the highest probability of occurrence.

THE STRUCTURE OF APPLICATION GROUPINGS FOR A TYPICAL INDUSTRIAL-SECTOR COMPANY

I.   Management and organization
        A.   Company and staff administrative services
                1.   Legal services
                2.   Insurance services
                3.   Stockholder services
                4.   Public relations
                5.   Library services
                6.   Warranty tracking services
                7.   Patent management
                8.   Mailing list services
                9.   Company store management services
        B.   Information processing services
                1.   Data entry, data collection, and data retrieval management
                2.   Program and application documentation control
                3.   System design, development, implementation, and analysis management
                4.   Data processing operations control and analysis
                5.   Intelligent workstation data and programming services
                6.   External and/or subsidiary data processing services
                7.   Systems and/or applications consulting services
                8.   Data and program security systems
        C.   Project management and control (internal)
                1.   Project scheduling and tracking
                2.   Facilities planning
                3.   Equipment planning
        D.   Office administrative services

1. Text processing services
2. In-house publishing services
3. Office systems management
4. Information retrieval systems management
5. Archival systems control
6. Internal communications management
7. Document and data capture systems management

E. Executive information services
   1. Query service of selected data
   2. Modeling service of queried data
   3. Business graphics service of modeled or queried data

II. Research/development/engineering
   A. Advanced engineering techniques services
      1. Operations research
      2. Mathematics and/or statistics
      3. Design graphics
      4. Discrete simulation
      5. Continuous simulation
      6. Mathematical modeling
      7. Network analysis
      8. Static analysis
      9. Dynamic analysis
      10. Physical property analysis
      11. Product property prediction analysis
      12. Raw material mix analysis
   B. Design engineering
      1. Engineering bill of material maintenance
      2. Engineering change control
      3. Product and project estimating and costing
      4. Engineering project management
      5. New or rework product definition and design
      6. Customer request for quote processing on engineered changes
      7. Technical data management
      8. Technical publications preparation
      9. Document and drawing creation, storage and distribution control
      10. Lofting systems management
      11. Inventory disposition (due to design changes) control

    C. Industrial and/or manufacturing engineering
1. Machine tool programming systems
2. Time and motion study analyses and controls
3. Line balancing systems
4. Nesting optimization systems
5. Variable length or mix optimization (from standard raw materials) systems
6. Routings creation and maintenance
7. Move, queue, run, and set-up time specification data maintenance
8. Machine and/or tool set-up specifications data maintenance
9. Tool and/or equipment design systems
10. Materials handling specifications data management
11. Manufacturing bill of material maintenance

    D. Quality control laboratory operations
1. Materials testing specifications and resultant data maintenance
2. Prototype testing data maintenance
3. Customer requested testing data maintenance
4. Process analysis and optimization systems
5. Scientific data management of quality control data
6. Yield analysis data systems
7. Testing of personnel material hazardous data maintenance

    E. Petroleum and/or mineral exploration and production
1. Geophysical data collection and reduction systems
2. Digital graphics systems for interpretive mapping

III. Personnel/training

    A. Personnel data management
1. Employment and recruitment data
2. Wage and salary administration controls
3. Employee services and benefits data
4. Skills inventory and analysis data
5. Industrial relations and union reporting plans and history
6. Non-payroll administration records maintenance
7. EEO government reporting data
8. Occupation hazard personnel history data
9. OSHA government reporting data
10. Personnel planning and scheduling data
11. Personnel performance planning and reporting

         12.   Personnel development programs

         13.   Retirement, separation, and leave of absence data

         14.   Attendance, illness, and vacation reporting data maintenance

  B.   Payroll data systems

         1.   Payroll creation

         2.   Tax deductions

         3.   Non-tax deductions

         4.   Tax (employee) government reporting

         5.   Electronic funds transfer (to employee)

         6.   Commission accounting

         7.   Donations accounting

         8.   Incentive pay accounting

         9.   Bonus program accounting

  C.   Training services

         1.   Data processing systems training

         2.   Data processing applications training

         3.   User workstation training

         4.   User application training

         5.   User office systems training

         6.   Internal and/or external education (seminar and conferences) scheduling and control

         7.   Internal development of education programs

         8.   Professional society promotions

IV.   Business and finance planning and accounting

  A.   Corporate planning

         1.   Strategic planning

         2.   Tactical planning

         3.   Operational planning

         4.   Economic research

  B.   Financial planning

         1.   Cash requirements analysis and planning

         2.   Cash investment analysis and planning

         3.   Tax planning

  C.   Financial management

         1.   Acquisition and venture planning

         2.   Competitive analysis

         3.   Capital projects planning

         4.   Investments tax analysis

         5.   Foreign operations accounting

      6.   Subsidiary accounting

      7.   Budget planning

  D.   Financial operations reporting

      1.   Government tax reporting

      2.   Budget reporting and control

      3.   Credit and short-term borrowing control

      4.   Cash management

  E.   General Accounting

      1.   General ledger and journal management

      2.   Accounts payable

      3.   Depreciation accounting

  F.   Customer accounting

      1.   Accounts receivable

      2.   Billing

      3.   Credit management

  G.   Cost accounting

      1.   Standard cost development

      2.   Cost accounting and control

      3.   Cost analysis

  H.   Asset accounting and control

      1.   Fixed asset accounting and control

      2.   Capital asset accounting and control

      3.   Lease asset accounting and control

  I.   Job costing

      1.   Product costing

      2.   Estimating and bidding

      3.   Services and off-site project accounting

  J.   Auditing

      1.   General auditing

      2.   Specific area auditing

V.   Physical asset management and control

  A.   Facilities and equipment control

      1.   Facilities and equipment planning and scheduling

      2.   Equipment cost and maintenance cost analysis systems

      3.   Property and facility management

  B.   Facilities and equipment maintenance

      1.   Maintenance work order and labor planning

      2.   Maintenance history and performance analysis

      3.   Maintenance cost accounting

      4. Maintenance parts management
      5. Preventive maintenance planning
      6. Maintaining equipment diagnostics
      7. On-line maintenance data collection
  C. Facilities management
      1. Physical building controlled access monitoring
      2. Services and power control
      3. Power demand optimization systems
      4. Energy conservation management
      5. Telephone and communication facilities management
  D. Environmental control
      1. Utility water and air purity control
      2. Environment monitoring
      3. Exhaust emission control
      4. Industrial plant waste control
      5. Continuous pollution control
      6. Batch pollution control
  E. Construction
      1. Management of plant construction
      2. Management of external construction contracts

VI. Material management
  A. Warehouse and stores
      1. Warehouse operations management
      2. Stores control
      3. Item location control
      4. Shelf space allocation control
      5. Order and requisition control
      6. Warehouse automation systems
      7. Distribution center operations control
      8. Bulk plant operations control
      9. Dealer and/or branch operations control
  B. Inventory control
      1. Raw materials accounting
      2. Purchased components accounting
      3. Work-in-process items accounting
      4. Finished goods accounting
      5. Service parts accounting
      6. Returned goods control
      7. Stock counting systems

       8.   Inventory accuracy accounting

       9.   Inventory valuation systems

     10.   Expendables control

     11.   Excess and obsolete inventory control

     12.   Scrap disposition control

     13.   Pick-and-move ticketing systems

  C. Purchasing and receiving

       1.   Purchase order creation and tracking data management

       2.   Receiving and receiving inspection systems

       3.   Receiving returns and unplanned receipts control

       4.   Quality assurance of purchased items data management

       5.   Expediting (purchases) control

       6.   Vendor evaluation and selection systems

       7.   Paperless receiving accounting (flow through receiving)

  D. Transport control

       1.   Internal material handling control

       2.   Inter plant and warehouse control

       3.   Pipeline transfer control

       4.   External subcontractor control and tracking

  E. Physical distribution

       1.   Tariff distribution planning and control

       2.   Freight bill rating and auditing

       3.   Shipping document preparation systems

       4.   Freight routing and consolidation optimization systems

       5.   Vehicle scheduling systems

VII. Merchandising and marketing

  A. Merchandising planning and control

       1.   Market environment analysis

       2.   Market research techniques

       3.   Distributor performance analysis

       4.   Sales statistics accounting

       5.   Sales force quota performance analysis

       6.   Sales forecasting

       7.   Product performance

       8.   Sales auditing

       9.   Commission plan development and analysis

     10.   New product requirements definition and analysis

     11.   Tracking sales marketed via external organizations

    B.   Sales promotion
- 1. Advertising planning and evaluation
- 2. Product introduction strategy
- 3. Promotion planning and evaluation
- 4. Contest planning and evaluation
- 5. Direct mailings
- 6. Sales promoted via external organizations

    C.   Order management
- 1. Order entry
- 2. Order entry route sales
- 3. Order processing
- 4. Order invoicing
- 5. Ordering tracking, handling order inquiries, and processing order changes
- 6. Credit authorization control
- 7. Point of sale data collection
- 8. Electronic funds transfer (from customer)
- 9. Sales (from product installation services) accounting
- 10. Customer data management

VIII.   Product planning and control

    A.   Master production schedule planning
- 1. Demand analysis planning
- 2. Planning bill of material maintenance
- 3. Master production planning
- 4. Master schedule planning

    B.   Material planning
- 1. Material requirements planning
- 2. Order release planning
- 3. Distribution requirements planning

    C.   Capacity planning
- 1. Resource planning (for total resources)
- 2. Rough-cut capacity planning (for key work centers)
- 3. Capacity requirements planning (for tomorrow's load by work center)

    D.   Plant rate planning
- 1. Final assembly end item planning and scheduling
- 2. Flow line rate planning

    E.   Plant operations

    1. Shop order tracking
    2. Flow line rate tracking
    3. Tool tracking
    4. Material tracking
    5. Labor reporting
    6. Production and scrap reporting
    7. Quality reporting
    8. Performance monitoring and evaluation
    9. Cost tracking and control

F. Plant support
    1. Work center analysis and control
    2. Tool center analysis and control
    3. Quality control administration control

APPENDIX II

TESTING THE DISAGGREGATION OF PRODUCT FAMILIES USING MIX PERCENTAGES

METHOD 1

Net demand period percentages applied to cumulative family net demand variances, with an inventory build up/run off calculation

1. *Assumption:* The family plan need not be level.
2. *Family production plan calculation*

	1	2	3	4	5	6
Source Plan	390	390	390	390	390	390
Net Family Demand	70	130	550	610	510	510
Period Variance	320	260	−160	−220	−120	−120
Cumulative Variance Family	320	580	420	200	80	−40
Adjust Quantity	0	0	+10	+10	+10	+10
Original Source Plan	390	390	390	390	390	390
New Production Plan	390	390	400	400	400	400
Net Family Demand	70	130	550	610	510	510
Period Variance	320	260	−150	−210	−110	−110
Cumulative Variance	320	580	430	220	110	0

3. *Family disaggregation to items*

Item 1	1	2	3	4	5	6
Cumulative Variance Family	320	580	430	220	110	0
Item %	0.43	0.62	0.18	0.26	0.12	0.12
Cumulative Variance Item	138	360	77	57	13	0
Inventory Build Up/Run Off	+138	+222	−283	−20	−44	−13
Item Demand	30	80	100	160	60	60
Item Production Plan	168	302	−183*	140	16	47

Item 2	1	2	3	4	5	6
Cumulative Variance Family	320	580	430	220	110	0
Item %	0	0	0.73	0.66	0.78	0.78
Cumulative Variance Item	0	0	314	145	86	0
Inventory Build Up/Run Off	0	0	+314	−169	−59	−86
Item Demand	0	0	400	400	400	400
Item Production Plan	0	0	714	231	341	314

Item 3	1	2	3	4	5	6
Cumulative Variance Family	320	580	430	220	110	0
Item %	0.57	0.31	0.05	0.03	0.02	0
Cumulative Variance Item	182	180	22	7	2	0
Inventory Build Up/Run Off	+ 182	− 2	− 158	− 15	− 5	− 2
Item Demand	40	40	30	20	10	0
Item Production Plan	222	38	− 128*	5	5	− 2*

Item 4	1	2	3	4	5	6
Cumulative Variance Family	320	580	430	220	110	0
Item %	0	0.07	0.04	0.05	0.08	0.10
Cumulative Variance Item	0	41	17	11	9	0
Inventory Build Up/Run Off	0	+ 41	− 24	− 6	− 2	− 9
Item Demand	0	10	20	30	40	50
Item Production Plan	0	51	− 4*	24	38	41

Summary

Item	1	2	3	4	5	6
1	168	302	− 183*	140	16	47
2	0	0	714	231	341	314
3	222	38	− 128*	5	5	− 2*
4	0	51	− 4*	24	38	41
Family	390	391	399	400	400	400

*Plans negative item production plans.

METHOD 2

Net demand percentages applied against period net demand family variances

1. *Assumption:* The family plan need not be level.
2. *Family production plan calculation*

	1	2	3	4	5	6
Source Plan	390	390	390	390	390	390
Net Family Demand	70	130	550	610	510	510
Period Variance Family	320	260	− 160	− 220	− 120	− 120
Cumulative Variance	320	580	420	200	80	− 40
Adjust Quantity	0	0	+ 10	+ 10	+ 10	+ 10
Original Source Plan	390	390	390	390	390	390
New Production Plan	390	390	400	400	400	400
Net Family Demand	70	130	550	610	510	510
Period Variance Family	320	260	− 150	− 210	− 110	− 110
Cumulative Variance	320	580	430	220	110	0

3. *Family disaggregation to items*

Item 1	1	2	3	4	5	6
Period Variance Family	320	260	− 150	− 210	− 110	− 110
Item %	0.43	0.62	0.18	0.26	0.12	0.12
Period Variance Item	138	161	− 27	− 55	− 13	− 13
Net Demand	30	80	100	160	60	60
Item Production Plan	168	241	73	105	47	47

Item 2	1	2	3	4	5	6
Period Variance Family	320	260	− 150	− 210	− 110	− 110
Item %	0	0	0.73	0.66	0.78	0.78
Period Variance Item	0	0	− 110	− 139	− 86	− 86
Net Demand	0	0	400	400	400	400
Item Production Plan	0	0	290	261	314	314

Item 3	1	2	3	4	5	6
Period Variance Family	320	260	− 150	− 210	− 110	− 110
Item %	0.57	0.31	0.05	0.03	0.02	0
Period Variance Item	182	81	− 8	− 6	− 2	− 0
Net Demand	40	40	30	20	10	0
Item Production Plan	222	121	22	14	8	0

Item 4	1	2	3	4	5	6
Period Variance Family	320	260	− 150	− 210	− 110	− 110
Item %	0	0.07	0.04	0.05	0.08	0.10
Period Variance Item	0	18	− 6	− 11	− 9	− 11
Net Demand	0	10	20	30	40	50
Item Production Plan	0	28	14	19	31	39

Summary

Item	1	2	3	4	5	6
1	168	241	73	105	47	47
2	0	0	290	261	314	314
3	222	121	22	14	8	0
4	0	28	14	19	31	39
Family	390	390	399	399	400	400

Notes:
ITEM
 (1) Net demand = 490; Plan = 681 − Excess.
 (2) Net demand = 1600; Plan = 1179 − Stockout.
 (3) Net demand = 140; Plan = 387 − Excess.
 (4) Net demand = 150; Plan = 131 − Stockout.
Plans do not equate to demand.

METHOD 3

Net demand horizon percentages applied against period net demand family variances

1. *Assumption:* The family plan need not be level.
2. *Family production plan calculation*

	1	2	3	4	5	6
Source Plan	390	390	390	390	390	390
Net Family Demand	70	130	550	610	510	510
Period Variance Family	320	260	− 160	− 220	− 120	− 120
Cumulative Variance	320	580	420	200	80	− 40
Adjust Quantity	0	0	+ 10	+ 10	+ 10	+ 10
Original Source Plan	390	390	390	390	390	390
New Production Plan	390	390	400	400	400	400
Net Family Demand	70	130	550	610	510	510
Period Variance Family	320	260	− 150	− 210	− 110	− 110
Cumulative Variance	320	580	430	220	110	0

3. *Family disaggregation to items*

Item 1	1	2	3	4	5	6
Period Variance Family	320	260	− 150	− 210	− 110	− 110
Item %	0.21	0.21	0.21	0.21	0.21	0.21
Period Variance Item	67	55	− 32	− 44	− 23	− 23
Net Demand	30	80	100	160	60	60
Item Production Plan	97	135	68	116	37	37

Item 2	1	2	3	4	5	6
Period Variance Family	320	260	− 150	− 210	− 110	− 110
Item %	0.67	0.67	0.67	0.67	0.67	0.67
Period Variance Item	214	174	− 101	− 141	− 74	− 74
Net Demand	0	0	400	400	400	400
Item Production Plan	214	174	299	259	326	326

Item 3	1	2	3	4	5	6
Period Variance Family	320	260	− 150	− 210	− 110	− 110
Item %	0.06	0.06	0.06	0.06	0.06	0.06
Period Variance Item	19	16	− 9	− 13	− 7	− 7
Net Demand	40	40	30	20	10	0
Item Production Plan	59	56	21	7	3	− 7*

Item 4	1	2	3	4	5	6
Period Variance Family	320	260	− 150	− 210	− 110	− 110
Item %	0.06	0.06	0.06	0.06	0.06	0.06
Period Variance Item	19	16	− 9	− 13	− 7	− 7
Net Demand	0	10	20	30	40	50
Item Production Plan	19	26	11	17	33	43

Summary

Item	1	2	3	4	5	6
1	97	135	86	116	37	37
2	214	174	299	259	326	326
3	59	56	21	7	3	− 7*
4	19	26	11	17	33	43
Family	389	391	399	399	399	399

*Plans negative quantities.

METHOD 4

Gross demand period percentages applied to cumulative family net demand variance with an inventory build up/run off calculation.

1. *Assumption:* The family plan need not be level.
2. *Family production plan calculation*

	1	2	3	4	5	6
Source Plan	390	390	390	390	390	390
Net Family Demand	70	130	550	610	510	510
Period Variance	320	260	− 160	− 220	− 120	− 120
Cumulative Variance Family	320	580	420	200	80	− 40
Adjust Quantity	0	0	+ 10	+ 10	+ 10	+ 10
Original Source Plan	390	390	390	390	390	390
New Production Plan	390	390	400	400	400	400
Net Family Demand	70	130	550	610	510	510
Period Variance	320	260	− 150	− 210	− 110	− 110
Cumulative Variance Family	320	580	430	220	110	0

3. *Family disaggregation to items*

Item 1	1	2	3	4	5	6
Cumulative Variance Family	320	580	430	220	110	0
Item %	0.12	0.15	0.18	0.26	0.12	0.12
Cumulative Variance Item	38	87	77	57	13	0
Inventory Build Up/Run Off	+ 38	+ 49	− 10	− 20	− 44	− 13
Item Demand	30	80	100	160	60	60
Item Production Plan	68	129	90	140	16	47

Item 2	1	2	3	4	5	6
Cumulative Variance Family	320	580	430	220	110	0
Item %	0.78	0.75	0.73	0.66	0.78	0.78
Cumulative Variance Item	250	435	314	145	86	0
Inventory Build Up/Run Off	+ 250	+ 185	− 121	− 169	− 59	− 86
Item Demand	0	0	400	400	400	400
Item Production Plan	250	185	279	231	341	314

Item 3	1	2	3	4	5	6
Cumulative Variance Family	320	580	430	220	110	0
Item %	0.10	0.08	0.05	0.03	0.02	0
Cumulative Variance Item	32	46	22	7	2	0
Inventory Build Up/Run Off	+32	+14	−24	−15	−5	−2
Item Demand	40	40	30	20	10	0
Item Production Plan	72	54	6	5	5	−2*

Item 4	1	2	3	4	5	6
Cumulative Variance Family	320	580	430	220	110	0
Item %	0	0.07	0.04	0.05	0.08	0.10
Cumulative Variance Item	0	12	17	11	9	0
Inventory Build Up/Run Off	0	+12	+5	−6	−2	−9
Item Demand	0	10	20	30	40	50
Item Production Plan	0	22	25	24	38	41

Summary

Item	1	2	3	4	5	6
1	68	129	90	140	16	47
2	250	184	279	231	341	314
3	72	54	6	5	5	−2*
4	0	22	25	24	38	41
Family	390	390	400	400	400	400

*Plans negative quantities.

METHOD 5

Gross demand period percentages applied against period net demand family variances.

1. *Assumption:* The family plan need not be level.
2. *Family production plan calculation*

	1	2	3	4	5	6
Source Plan	390	390	390	390	390	390
Net Family Demand	70	130	550	610	510	510
Period Variance Family	320	260	− 160	− 220	− 120	− 120
Cumulative Variance	320	580	420	200	80	− 40
Adjust Quantity	0	0	+ 10	+ 10	+ 10	+ 10
Original Source Plan	390	390	390	390	390	390
New Production Plan	390	390	400	400	400	400
Net Family Demand	70	130	550	610	510	510
Period Variance Family	320	260	− 150	− 210	− 110	− 110
Cumulative Variance	320	580	430	220	110	0

3. *Family disaggregation to items*

Item 1	1	2	3	4	5	6
Period Variance Family	320	260	− 150	− 210	− 110	− 110
Item %	0.12	0.15	0.18	0.26	0.12	0.12
Period Variance Item	38	39	− 27	− 55	− 13	− 13
Net Demand	30	80	100	160	60	60
Item Production Plan	68	119	73	105	47	47

Item 2	1	2	3	4	5	6
Period Variance Family	320	260	− 150	− 210	− 110	− 110
Item %	0.78	0.75	0.73	0.66	0.78	0.78
Period Variance Item	250	195	− 110	− 139	− 86	− 86
Net Demand	0	0	400	400	400	400
Item Production Plan	250	195	290	261	314	314

Item 3	1	2	3	4	5	6
Period Variance Family	320	260	−150	−210	−110	−110
Item %	0.10	0.08	0.05	0.03	0.02	0
Period Variance Item	32	21	−8	−6	−2	0
Net Demand	40	40	30	20	10	0
Item Production Plan	72	61	22	14	8	0

Item 4	1	2	3	4	5	6
Period Variance Family	320	260	−150	−210	−110	−110
Item %	0	0.02	0.04	0.05	0.08	0.10
Period Variance Item	0	5	−6	−11	−9	−11
Net Demand	0	10	20	30	40	50
Item Production Plan	0	15	14	19	31	39

Summary

Item	1	2	3	4	5	6
1	68	119	73	105	47	47
2	250	195	290	261	314	314
3	72	61	22	14	8	0
4	0	15	14	19	31	39
Family	390	390	399	399	400	400

Notes:
ITEM
  (1) Net demand = 490; Plan = 459 − Stockout.
  (2) Net demand = 1600; Plan = 1624 − Excess.
  (3) Net demand = 140; Plan = 177 − Excess.
  (4) Net demand = 150; Plan = 118 − Stockout.

METHOD 6

Gross demand period percentages applied against period gross demand family variances.

1. *Assumption:* The family plan should be level.
2. *Family production plan calculation*

	1	2	3	4	5	6	7	8	9	10	11	12
Family Production Plan	600	600	600	600	600	600	600	600	600	600	600	600
Gross Demand Family	510	530	550	610	510	510	520	520	530	530	540	540
Period Variance Family	90	70	50	−10	90	90	80	80	70	70	60	60
Cumulative Variance	90	160	210	200	290	380	460	540	610	680	740	800
Adjust Quantity	−50	−50	−50	−50	−50	−50	−50	−50	−50	−50	−50	−50
Family Production Plan	600	600	600	600	600	600	600	600	600	600	600	600
New Family Production Plan	550	550	550	550	550	550	550	550	550	550	550	550
Gross Demand Family	510	530	550	610	510	510	520	520	530	530	540	540
Period Variance	40	20	0	−60	40	40	30	30	20	20	10	10
Cumulative Variance	40	60	60	0	40	80	110	140	160	180	190	200

3. *Family disaggregation to items*

Item 1

	1	2	3	4	5	6	7	8	9	10	11	12
Period Variance Family	40	20	0	−60	40	40	30	30	20	20	10	10
Item %	0.12	0.15	0.18	0.26	0.12	0.12	0.12	0.10	0.10	0.10	0.11	0.11
Period Variance Item	5	3	0	−16	5	5	4	3	2	2	1	1
Gross Demand Item	60	80	100	160	60	60	60	50	50	50	60	60
Gross Item Production Plan	65	83	100	144	65	65	64	53	52	52	61	61

Item 2

	1	2	3	4	5	6	7	8	9	10	11	12
Period Variance Family	40	20	0	−60	40	40	30	30	20	20	10	10
Item %	0.78	0.75	0.73	0.66	0.78	0.78	0.77	0.77	0.75	0.75	0.74	0.74
Period Variance Item	31	15	0	−40	31	31	23	23	15	15	7	7
Gross Demand Item	400	400	400	400	400	400	400	400	400	400	400	400
Gross Item Production Plan	431	415	400	360	431	431	423	423	415	415	407	407

Item 3

	1	2	3	4	5	6	7	8	9	10	11	12
Period Variance Family	40	20	0	−60	40	40	30	30	20	20	10	10
Item %	0.10	0.08	0.05	0.03	0.02	0	0	0	0	0	0	0
Period Variance Item	4	2	0	−2	1	0	0	0	0	0	0	0
Gross Demand Item	50	40	30	20	10	0	0	0	0	0	0	0
Gross Item Production Plan	54	42	30	18	11	0	0	0	0	0	0	0

Item 4

	1	2	3	4	5	6	7	8	9	10	11	12
Period Variance Family	40	20	0	−60	40	40	30	30	20	20	10	10
Item %	0	0.02	0.04	0.05	0.08	0.10	0.11	0.13	0.15	0.15	0.15	0.15
Period Variance Item	0	0	0	−3	3	4	3	4	3	3	2	2
Gross Demand Item	0	10	20	30	40	50	60	70	80	80	80	80
Gross Item Production Plan	0	10	20	27	43	54	63	74	83	83	82	82

4. *Inventory projection*

Item 1	1	2	3	4	5	6	7	8	9	10	11	12
Inventory	30	30	33	33	17	22	27	31	34	36	38	39
Production	65	83	100	144	65	65	64	53	52	52	61	61
Total Available	95	113	133	177	82	87	91	84	86	88	99	100
Demand	60	80	100	160	60	60	60	50	50	50	60	60
Inventory Remaining	30	33	33	17	22	27	31	34	36	38	39	40

Item 2	1	2	3	4	5	6	7	8	9	10	11	12
Inventory	800	831	846	846	806	837	868	891	914	929	944	951
Production	431	415	400	360	431	431	423	423	415	415	407	407
Total Available	1231	1246	1246	1206	1237	1268	1291	1314	1329	1344	1351	1358
Demand	400	400	400	400	400	400	400	400	400	400	400	400
Inventory Remaining	831	846	846	806	837	868	891	914	929	944	951	958

Item 3	1	2	3	4	5	6	7	8	9	10	11	12
Inventory	10	14	16	16	14	15	15	15	15	15	15	15
Production	54	42	30	18	11	0	0	0	0	0	0	0
Total Available	64	56	46	34	25	15	15	15	15	15	15	15
Demand	50	40	30	20	10	0	0	0	0	0	0	0
Inventory Remaining	14	16	16	14	15	15	15	15	15	15	15	15

Item 4	1	2	3	4	5	6	7	8	9	10	11	12
Inventory	0	0	0	0	-3	0	4	7	11	14	17	19
Production	0	10	20	27	43	54	63	74	83	83	82	82
Total Available	0	10	20	27	40	54	67	81	94	97	99	101
Demand	0	10	20	30	40	50	60	70	80	80	80	80
Inventory Remaining	0	0	0	-3	0	4	7	11	14	17	19	21

Note:
ITEM
(1) In all cases, inventory increases.
(2) Item 4 has a planned stockout in period 4.

METHOD 7

Gross demand horizon percentages applied against period net demand family variances.

1. *Assumption:* The family plan need not be level.
2. *Family production plan calculation*

	1	2	3	4	5	6
Source Plan	390	390	390	390	390	390
Net Family Demand	70	130	550	610	510	510
Period Variance Family	320	260	− 160	− 220	− 120	− 120
Cumulative Variance	320	580	420	200	80	− 40
Adjust Quantity	0	0	+ 10	+ 10	+ 10	+ 10
Original Source Plan	390	390	390	390	390	390
New Production Plan	390	390	400	400	400	400
Net Family Demand	70	130	550	610	510	510
Period Variance Family	320	260	− 150	− 210	− 110	− 110
Cumulative Variance	320	580	430	220	110	0

3. *Family disaggregation to items*

Item 1	1	2	3	4	5	6
Period Variance Family	320	260	− 150	− 210	− 110	− 110
Item %	0.15	0.15	0.15	0.15	0.15	0.15
Period Variance Item	48	39	− 23	− 32	− 17	− 17
Net Demand	30	80	100	160	60	60
Item Production Plan	78	119	77	128	43	43

Item 2	1	2	3	4	5	6
Period Variance Family	320	260	− 150	− 210	− 110	− 110
Item %	0.75	0.75	0.75	0.75	0.75	0.75
Period Variance Item	240	195	− 113	− 158	− 83	− 83
Net Demand	0	0	400	400	400	400
Item Production Plan	240	195	287	242	317	317

Item 3	1	2	3	4	5	6
Period Variance Family	320	260	− 150	− 210	− 110	− 110
Item %	0.05	0.05	0.05	0.05	0.05	0.05
Period Variance Item	16	13	− 8	− 11	− 6	− 6
Net Demand	40	40	30	20	10	0
Item Production Plan	56	53	22	9	4	− 6*

Item 4	1	2	3	4	5	6
Period Variance Family	320	260	− 150	− 210	− 110	− 110
Item %	0	0.05	0.05	0.05	0.05	0.05
Period Variance Item	16	13	− 8	− 11	− 6	− 6
Net Demand	0	10	20	30	40	50
Item Production Plan	16	23	12	19	34	44

Summary

Item	1	2	3	4	5	6
1	78	119	77	128	43	43
2	240	195	287	242	317	317
3	56	53	22	9	4	− 6*
4	16	23	12	19	34	44
Family	390	390	398	398	398	398

*Plans negative quantities.

METHOD 8

Gross demand horizon percentages applied against family production plan quantities.

1. *Assumption:* The family plan need not be level.

2. *Family production plan calculation*

	1	2	3	4	5	6
Source Plan	390	390	390	390	390	390
Net Family Demand	70	130	550	610	510	510
Period Variance	320	260	−160	−220	−120	−120
Cumulative Variance Family	320	580	420	200	80	−40
Adjust Quantity	0	0	+10	+10	+10	+10
Original Source Plan	390	390	390	390	390	390
New Production Plan	390	390	400	400	400	400
Net Family Demand	70	130	550	610	510	510
Period Variance	320	260	−150	−210	−110	−110
Cumulative Variance	320	580	430	220	110	0

3. *Family disaggregation to items*

Item 1	1	2	3	4	5	6
Family Production Plan	390	390	400	400	400	400
Item %	0.15	0.15	0.15	0.15	0.15	0.15
Gross Production Plan	59	59	60	60	60	60

Item 2	1	2	3	4	5	6
Family Production Plan	390	390	400	400	400	400
Item %	0.75	0.75	0.75	0.75	0.75	0.75
Gross Item Production Plan	293	293	300	300	300	300

Item 3	1	2	3	4	5	6
Family Production Plan	390	390	400	400	400	400
Item %	0.05	0.05	0.05	0.05	0.05	0.05
Gross Item Production Plan	20	20	20	20	20	20

Item 4	1	2	3	4	5	6
Family Production Plan	390	390	400	400	400	400
Item %	0.05	0.05	0.05	0.05	0.05	0.05
Gross Item Production Plan	20	20	20	20	20	20

Summary

Item	1	2	3	4	5	6
1	59	59	60	60	60	60
2	293	293	300	300	300	300
3	20	20	20	20	20	20
4	20	20	20	20	20	20
Family	392	392	400	400	400	400

Note:
ITEM
(1) Net Demand = 490; Plan = 358 − Inv. 30 = 328 − Stockout.
(2) Net Demand = 1600; Plan = 1786 − Inv. 800 = 986 − Stockout.
(3) Net Demand = 140; Plan = 120 − Inv. 10 = 110 − Stockout.
(4) Net Demand = 150; Plan = 120 − Inv. 0 = 120 − Stockout.

METHOD 9

Gross demand period percentages applied against period gross demand family variances and adjusted by inventory.

1. *Assumption:* The production plan may start level.
2. *Family production plan calculation*

	1	2	3	4	5	6	7	8	9	10	11	12
Production Plan	600	600	600	600	600	600	600	600	600	600	600	600
Demand Plan	510	530	550	610	510	510	520	520	530	530	540	540
Period Variance Family	90	70	50	−10	90	90	80	80	70	70	60	60
Inventory	840											
Cumulative Variance	390	1000	1050	1040	1130	1220	1300	1380	1450	1520	1580	1640

	1	2	3	4	5	6	7	8	9	10	11	12
Base Plan	600	600	600	600	600	600	600	600	600	600	600	600
Adjust Quantity	−136	−136	−136	−136	−136	−136	−136	−136	−136	−136	−136	−136
Operating Plan	464	464	464	464	464	464	464	464	464	464	464	464
Gross Family Demand	510	530	550	610	510	510	520	520	530	530	540	540
Period Variance Family	−46	−66	−86	−146	−46	−46	−56	−56	−66	−66	−76	−76
Inventory	840											
Cumulative Variance	794	728	642	496	450	404	348	292	226	160	84	8

3. Family disaggregation to items

Item 1	1	2	3	4	5	6
Period Variance Family	− 46	− 66	− 86	− 146	− 46	− 46
Item %	0.13	0.13	0.13	0.13	0.13	0.13
Period Variance Item	− 6	− 9	− 11	− 19	− 6	− 6
Gross Demand	60	80	100	160	60	60
Item Production Plan	54	71	89	141	54	54

Item 2	1	2	3	4	5	6
Period Variance Family	− 46	− 66	− 86	− 146	− 46	− 46
Item %	0.75	0.75	0.75	0.75	0.75	0.75
Period Variance Item	− 35	− 50	− 65	− 100	− 35	− 35
Gross Demand	400	400	400	400	400	400
Item Production Plan	365	350	335	290	365	365

Item 3	1	2	3	4	5	6
Period Variance Family	− 46	− 66	− 86	− 146	− 46	− 46
Item %	0.02	0.02	0.02	0.02	0.02	0.02
Period Variance Item	− 1	− 1	− 2	− 3	− 1	− 1
Gross Demand	50	40	30	20	10	0
Item Production Plan	49	39	28	17	9	− 1*

Item 4	1	2	3	4	5	6
Period Variance Family	− 46	− 66	− 86	− 146	− 46	− 46
Item %	0.10	0.10	0.10	0.10	0.10	0.10
Period Variance Item	− 5	− 7	− 9	− 15	− 5	− 5
Gross Demand	0	10	20	30	40	50
Item Production Plan	− 5*	3	11	15	35	45

Summary

Item	1	2	3	4	5	6
1	54	71	89	141	54	54
2	365	350	337	290	365	365
3	49	35	28	17	9	− 1*
4	− 5*	3	11	15	35	45
Family	463	463	463	463	463	463

*Plans negative quantities.

APPENDIX III

GLOSSARY OF TERMS

Actual sales   Booked customer orders for shipment now or in the future. If the promised shipping date is past due, then the shipping date is considered to be the current date.

Adjusted production forecast   A production forecast that may have been derived via statistical methods and has been adjusted by extrinsic values and management goals.

Aggregate   To put together, as to put together all of the item requirements into family requirements. Normally refers to summing the item level data to a product or production family level of data.

Allocation   The designation of a specific quantity of a specific item to be utilized. If time is involved, it is sometimes called time phased allocation.

Anticipated demand   A projection of what sales or consumption of the product will probably amount to. A forecast or blended demand.

Assembly line   A manufacturing process wherein subassemblies and/or components are assembled. It may be a flow line.

ATP   See **Available to promise.**

Available inventory   Inventory that is available for calculating net demand. In MPSP it is usually equal to on-hand inventory minus safety stock minus hedged inventory. (Allocations are not considered.)

Available resources   The plant capacities of machines and labor in terms of hours or cost that are available for scheduling or allocating. There may be other resources, such as square feet or floor space.

Available to promise   That quantity of committed production that is not yet committed to a sale. It is available to promise to a customer.

Balance on hand   An inventory calculation of how many of the item exist for whatever reason. (Normally the total on hand.)

Bill of material   The material (raw material, purchased parts, fabricated parts, subassemblies, etc.) that are used to produce the product. Sometimes structured as a total list, a partial list (as those things required for the next level of assembly), or an indented structure list.

Blend   To combine, by whatever mix, actual sales and forecasted sales.

Blended demand   The anticipated demand that has been blended (actual sales and forecasted sales have been merged) to produce a more accurate picture of what sales will actually occur.

BOH   See **Balance on hand.**

Booked order   A sales order for a product that has been accepted for shipment on a specific date.

Bucket   A planning period. A bucket may be any grouping of time, such as a day, a week, a month, a quarter, a semi-annual period, a year, or a number of years. Buckets vary in size according to what function does the planning. For example, MPP may use months, MSP may use weeks, and MRP may use days.

Business plan   A statement of income projections, costs, and profits usually accompanied by budgets and a projected balance sheet as well as a cash-flow (source and application of funds) statement. It is usually stated in monetary terms.

Business planning   The process of converting the business plan into gross level projections for input to forecasting.

Capacity   The amount of time that a resource is available for scheduling. For example, a machine that operates eight hours per day for five days per week has a weekly capacity of 40 hours.

Capacity requirements planning   A detailed plan of required work center capacity based on individual piece part planning, as dictated by MRP and shop routing files. The approach is to "simulate" the work flow at each machine center based on all open orders plus all planned orders, thereby creating a period-by-period profile of expected capacity requirements at each work center.

CMLT   See **Cumulative manufacturing lead time** and **Cumulative material lead time.** The abbreviation often applies to both, and since each has a different meaning, it should be defined when used.

Cumulative manufacturing lead time   The cumulative manufacturing lead time through all lower levels of an item's product structure. It is the sum of the planned lead times through the longest path of component product structure levels. It includes the lead time for the item itself. Sometimes used as a planning time fence.

Cumulative material lead time   The same as the cumulative manufacturing lead time with the purchasing procurement cycle added.

Composite resource profile   A resource profile that is composed of two or more other profiles. The total resources required to produce one of a specific item.

COS   See **Customer order servicing.**

Cost planning and control The functional area for maintaining all product costs. Includes data accumulation, calculation, and reporting.

CRP See **Capacity requirements planning.**

Current item plans Those item production plans that are currently being produced. Sometimes referred to as operational item plans. When lot sized, these plans are MSP orders.

Customer demand The sales demand imposed upon a manufacturing company by a customer. May be an actual sale, a forecast, or a blend of actual sales and a forecast.

Customer order An order for a particular product or a number of products from a customer. Often referred to as "actual sales" to distinguish it from "forecasted sales."

Customer order servicing The manufacturing functional area that covers all aspects of the entry, processing, and managing of a customer order.

Data element An element of information stored by a computer. One or more data elements make up a record. One or more records make up a file.

Demand The need for a particular product or item. The demand can come from a number of sources, such as actual sales, forecasted sales, or service part requirements.

Demand analysis The process of accepting a variety of demand sources as input, sifting those to models, options, production level items, and so forth, applying the option to blend with actual sales, and producing net demand for master production planning and/or master schedule planning.

Demand analysis planning The process of accomplishing the MPSP subfunction demand analysis. See **Demand analysis.** Often not performed as a separate subfunction, but accomplished in conjunction with master production planning and master schedule planning.

Demand identification The process of defining the demand source for an item that will be identified as gross demand and, after netting to inventory, as net demand.

Demand Management A major manufacturing function that may or may not (depending on the user) include forecasting, order entry, supply (inventory) analysis, and demand analysis.

Demand time fence A planning technique used to identify specific periods wherein some planning action is to take place, such as in blending.

Disaggregate To take apart. Normally refers to taking product (production) family data apart to item level data. Uses mix percentages to identify the portion of family data that applies to a specific item. Works best with a family of items that have identical sales trends.

Display To present for viewing. A display of information may be on a report or on a terminal. A display is also a terminal with a cathode ray tube, liquid crystal, gas panel, or some other type of viewing screen.

DTF See **Demand time fence.**

End item   The product that ships to the customer. May or may not be the item that is planned in MPSP.

Engineering and production data control   A grouping of manufacturing functions including bill-of-material processing, routing data management, and facilities data management.

E & PDC   See **Engineering and production data control.**

Explode   To take apart a structure level by level to identify the components that make up the structure. Product structures and sales families are often exploded in order to be used.

Explode models   If product structures contain models underneath which are options and/or variants, this is the process used to identify the required quantity of the options and/or variants. For example, given a forecasted quantity for a model, an option quantity would be equal to the model quantity times the option percentage applicable. The percentage should remain relatively constant for this process to be effective.

Explode product structure   To take apart a product structure to identify the components that make up the structure. No percentages are used unless models are encountered in the structure. The structure usually represents how the product is manufactured or assembled.

Explode sales family   Sales families are normally groups of items with similar sales trends. The grouping is done so that the family can be forecasted instead of all of the individual items. Percentages are used to identify how much of the family forecast is applicable to any specific item. The percentages are often average horizon percentages.

Facility data management   The process of maintaining the data on the plant floor for machine and labor, hours, and costs.

Family   A grouping of items. See **Sales family and product family.**

Family production plan   The quantity per period by production family that management desires to produce. The family production plan may be adjusted by management.

Family profile   See **Family resource profile.**

Family resource profile   The resources across the planning periods that are required to produce theoretical one of the family. It is usually based on the percentage of each item's resource profile that makes up the family.

FAS   See **Final assembly schedule.**

Flow line/flow shop   A manufacturing process wherein all of manufacturing steps/operations are in line. Characteristics are high-volume products, minimum product options, minimum work queues, and single item (or small lot) transport.

Final assembly schedule   Also referred to as a "finishing schedule" because it may include operations other than just assembly operations. It is a schedule of end items either to replenish finish goods inventory or to finish the product for a make-to-order product. For make-to-order products, it is prepared after receipt of a customer order, is constrained by the availability of material and capacity, and it schedules the operations required to complete the product from the level where it is stocked (or master scheduled) to the end item level.

Firm planned order   A planned order than can be frozen in quantity and time. The computer is not allowed to automatically change it since this is the responsibility of the scheduler in charge of the item that is being planned. This technique helps schedulers working with MPSP to manage material and capacity problems by firming up selected planned orders.

Forecasting   A manufacturing function used to predict sales. May be intrinsic, as with statistical analysis of historical sales, or extrinsic, as with the application of economic trends or a combination of both. See **Gross demand** for examples of what can be forecasted.

Forecasted sales   See **Sales forecast** or **Forecasting.**

Gross demand   Demand that has not been netted against available inventory. Gross demand may exist for any of the following to satisfy the needs of customers, sister plants, and distribution centers.

A sales family forecast

An end item forecast

A model forecast

An option forecast

A service part forecast

Actual end item sales

Actual model sales

Actual option sales

Actual service part sales

Hedge   To build ahead. Used in production planning to level the planned quantities. For example, if a demand spike exists in the future that exceeds production capacity, earlier periods may build more than is required in those periods to accommodate the demand spike in the future period.

Hedged inventory   That inventory which has been built ahead to satisfy a demand in a future period. Hedged inventory must be managed separately to avoid its consumption in the net demand calculation for a period where it was not planned to be consumed. Sometimes referred to as held inventory.

Horizon   The time distance into the future. For example, a three-year horizon means that the plan will extend across the next three years.

IA   See **Inventory accounting.**

IM   See **Inventory management.**

Inventory accounting   A manufacturing function which maintains the inventory status on any item. It identifies how many of an item are where. It also identifies if they are safety stock, are allocated to an order, are hedged inventory items, or are available for sale or netting against gross demand.

Inventory management   A major manufacturing function that normally includes inventory accounting, material requirements planning, and inventory analysis subsystems.

Inventory status   That which is maintained by inventory accounting. See **Inventory accounting.**

Item   A general term referring to a model, option, production planning item, or master schedule item. It may be a product or some level below the product level in structure. It may have been exploded from a sales family.

Item demand   The gross or net demand for an item. See **Item** and **Demand.**

Item orders   The planned period production quantities for an item that have been lot sized into specific planned orders for release from MSP to MRP.

Item production plan   The quantity per period by item that management desires to produce.

Item resource profile   The resources (material/machine/labor) in terms of units/dollars across time that are required to produce one of an item.

Item sales forecast   The forecast for an individual item. The item may be structured into a sales family (with an associated sales family forecast) and additionally have a direct item sales forecast, such as for service requirements (which may have a totally different forecast trend and prepared by different personnel).

Job shop   A manufacturing process wherein similar machines are grouped together into work centers. Normally requires the components for a specific product to be routed back and forth between these work centers. Characteristics are often models/options, large queues, setup considerations, long wait times in the manufacturing cycle and custom products.

Labor capacity   That amount of labor, normally in terms of hours or costs for some period, which is available for scheduling.

Lead time   The time that is required to produce a product or component. See **Cumulative manufacturing lead time** and **Cumulative material lead time.**

Lot size   The quantity to be produced on a shop work order. The quantity is often a balance between the cost to set up a machine to run the item and the cost to store excess items that do not have immediate demand. A lot size may be for a quantity of one or more.

Machine capacity   The amount of time which a machine, in terms of hours and costs for some period, is available for scheduling.

Machine set up   The process of preparing a machine to make a specific part. Machine set-up time is a key consideration in establishing the lot size or run quantity (once the machine is set up). Strong emphasis is currently being applied to reduce set-up times from hours to minutes and thereby reduce lot size quantities to single items.

Master level item An item that is going to be managed by MPSP. It can be at any level in the product structure. See **Master schedule item.**

Master production planning The function of setting the overall level of manufacturing output. Its prime purpose is to establish production rates that will achieve management's objective in terms of raising or lowering inventories or backlogs, while usually attempting to keep the production force relatively stable. The production plan is usually stated in broad terms as families of products, and must extend through a planning horizon sufficient to plan the labor, equipment facilities, material, and finances required to accomplish the production plan. Various units of measure are used by different companies to express the plan, such as standard hours, tonnage, labor operators, units, pieces, dollars, and so on. As this plan affects all company functions, it is normally prepared with information from Marketing, Manufacturing, Engineering, Finance, Material Planning, and so on. It is management's strategy to meet the net demand for an item while making the best use of production capacity.

Master production schedule For selected MLI items, it is a statement of what the company expects to manufacture. It is the anticipated build schedule for those selected items assigned to the master scheduler. The master scheduler maintains this schedule and, in turn, it becomes a set of planning numbers which "drives" MRP. It represents what the company plans to produce expressed in specific configurations, quantities, and dates.

Master production schedule planning A key manufacturing function which provides input to inventory management. Consists of three major areas: demand analysis, master production planning, and master schedule planning.

Master scheduler The job title of the person who manages the master production schedule. This person should be the best scheduler available, as the consequences of the planning done here has a great impact on material and capacity planning. Ideally, the person would have a substantial product and shop knowledge.

Master schedule item An item selected to be planned by the master scheduler. The item is deemed critical in terms of its impact on lower-level components and/or resources such as skilled labor, key machines, dollars, critical suppliers, and so forth. Therefore, the master scheduler, not the computer, maintains the plan for these items.

Master schedule planning The process of using the item production plan from master production planning or manually entered data to derive a master schedule of orders that will satisfy an item production plan.

Material requirements planning The manufacturing process of accepting master schedule orders as requirements and exploding them through the product structure to plan all material and components requirements in the proper time frame.

MLI   See **Master level item.**

Model   An item that consists of one or more options, variants, and standard parts. Models may be planned by using option/variant percentages, but they usually are not stocked. Normally, models are assembled based on customer selections of options and variants.

Model structure   A structure depicting the options and variants within a model. Options and variants have associated percentages of usage within the model. The structure may be referred to as a planning bill of material.

MPP   See **Master production planning.**

MPS   See **Master production schedule.**

MPSP   See **Master production schedule planning.**

MRP   See **Material requirements planning.**

MSP   See **Master schedule planning.**

Net demand/net item demand   Gross demand minus safety stock and hedge inventory for MPSP calculations. Allocations are usually not considered in the net demand calculation for MPSP. The calculation may be spread across multiple planning periods. Net item demands must be known before net family demands can be calculated.

Offset   Used in the development of an item resource profile to determine the resources that would be consumed in periods prior to the product completion period. Offsets are negative, backed off from some defined period in the future.

Operational management   The management in a manufacturing company that makes the day-to-day decisions on running the company.

Option   A choice. A feature of an end product, usually specified by the customer. Every option has a percentage of usage on the model. If multiple options are available for a model, the option percentages do not have to add up to 100%. Sometimes the word option is used as a common term meaning both an option and a variant.

Option demand   See **Option sales forecast.**

Option sales forecast   The forecast for individual options. This category is provided so that forecast data can be prepared for:

> Options that are not grouped into a model/option structure
> Options that are sold to meet service requirements

Order entry   The process of accepting and translating what a customer wants into terms used by the computer. This can be as simple as creating shipping documents for a finished goods product line, to a more complicated series of activities including engineering effort for make-to-order products. A subfunction of customer order servicing.

Order promising   See **Available to promise.** The process of making a delivery commitment, that is, answering the question "When can you ship?" For make-to-order products this usually involves a check of uncommitted material and the availability of capacity.

PCM   See **Production control manager.**

Period   A time bucket, which may be a day, week, month, and so on. See **Bucket.**

Planned inventory   The desired amount of inventory that is planned to exist for each period as a result of the production plan incremental values, the running balances and the demand plan.

Planned orders   Within the framework of planned, firm, and open orders, planned orders are those that are normally managed by the scheduling system. The system may recalculate dates and required quantities at any time on a planned order.

Planned production   The anticipated production that was derived through testing against production targets and/or available resources for product families or items.

Plant flow line scheduling   Flow line manufacturing is usually a continuous process that is based on desired period rates as opposed to shop orders. Flow line scheduling therefore is the utilization of a rate schedule, such as a daily going rate.

Plant maintenance   A manufacturing function which addresses the total maintenance of the plant (machines, building, air conditioning, and so on) from both a preventive and remedial maintenance standpoint.

Plant monitoring and control   A manufacturing function which addresses what machines should be producing what components and also records what machines actually are producing what components. May be automated (sensors hooked directly on the machines) or require machine operator input to record actual performance.

PM   See **Preventive maintenance.**

PM & C   See **Plant monitoring and control.**

Preventive maintenance   The process of keeping a maintenance schedule on machines and equipment to prevent breakdowns. Normally includes spare parts inventory management and can include personnel scheduling by skill classification.

Product   The end item, or that which is sold. It is not necessarily an MPSP item.

Product family   May be called a production family. A grouping of items to allow for MPP to be performed with greater ease. Items may be structured into product families for any reason, such as resources, materials, costs, and so on. Items that are structured into product families are not necessarily end items.

Product group   A grouping of items. May be a sales family or a product family.

Product supply plan   The gross demand plan prepared by management for a family/model/option/item that may or may not have any relationship to forecast data. It is represented as a quantity per period.

Production control manager   That person responsible for meeting demand with production on a day-to-day basis. May or may not have input to MPP.

Production family   A structure of one or more models/options/items into a single level (Level 0, Level 1) structure to facilitate the production planning process. See **Product family.**

Production family net demand   The sum of the item net demand for all items within the production (product) family per time period.

Production plan   The agreed-upon strategy that comes from the production planning function. See **Production planning.**

Production planner   The person who works with the master production plan to manage it. He or she meets with top and operational management to insure that the resultant plan is desired and achievable.

Production planning   Two meanings exist.

> The process of managing the master (family level) production plan.
>
> The process of managing the day-to-day item production levels against current demands.

Production schedule   The same as the production plan. See **Production planning.**

Production target   A quantity per period for a product family that may be established by:

> An estimate by management, which may or may not be achievable
>
> A desire by management to drive the business (on multiple product lines) in a specific direction
>
> An actual calculation wherein the targets are input as net demands to the MPSP process

Projected sales   A forecast or estimate of what sales will be in the future. See **Forecasting.**

Purchasing   A manufacturing function that includes subfunctions, such as requisition processing, purchase order preparation, vendor analysis, purchase order acknowledgement control, open purchase order control, and purchase order tracking.

Queue   In manufacturing, this is a work-in process buildup. A queue can exist on the input or output of an operation. The input is parts waiting to be worked on. The output is parts waiting to be moved to the next operation or work center. Large queues cause large work-in process inventories. Job shops tend to have larger queues than flow shops.

RCCP   See **Rough-cut capacity planning.**

Receiving   A manufacturing function that provides for netting the receipts of materials from vendors against the originally issued purchase orders. It accommodates partial shipments, overshipments, and rejections.

Remedial maintenance   That maintenance which is performed because the machine/equipment is no longer operational. A remedial maintenance system should interface with the preventive maintenance system.

Resource   Relates to an available capacity. A required resource may be machinery, tools, labor, space, funds, or any other requirement. The lack of a resource in a planning period will constrain production in that period.

Resource planning   An MPSP function which is often referred to as resource requirements planning when it relates to master production planning, and rough-cut capacity planning when it relates to master schedule planning. The objective is to ascertain if the planning quantities can actually be produced by the available resources.

Resource profile   A statement of the key resources needed to manufacture one unit of an item or a family. Used for resource testing in master production planning as a family resource profile, and in master schedule planning as an item resource profile.

Resource requirements planning   Resource planning at the master production planning level which is done long term on total requirements.

Resource testing   The process of converting the master production plan and/or the master production schedule plan into the impact on key resources, such as labor hours, machine hours, storage, standard cost dollars, shipping dollars, inventory levels, and so forth. Resource profiles are used to accomplish this testing. The purpose is to evaluate the plan prior to attempting to implement it. This is not to be confused with CRP, which is a detailed review of capacity requirements.

RM   See **Remedial maintenance.**

RRP   See **Resource requirements planning.**

Rough-cut capacity planning   Resource planning at the master schedule planning level which is done short term on critical work center requirements.

Routing   The sequence of operations through various work centers that have to be performed in order to produce the item. Flow shops tend to have fixed routings while job shops tend to have variable routings.

Routing data management   A manufacturing function that manages all routing data. Provides for routing data maintenance with additions, deletions and changes. It also allows "same as except" copies, and generic routing maintenance.

Safety stock   Additional inventory planned as protection, typically against forecast errors and/or short-term changes in the backlog. This investment is often under the control of the master scheduler, in terms of when it should be planned.

Sales family A grouping of one or more items that have similar sales trends into a single level (or sometimes a multiple level) structure so that a forecast can be prepared for the family instead of for all the individual items.

Sales forecast What Marketing plans to sell. It is a forecast of sales (family/model/option/item), which is stated by the period in which the shipment is to be made.

Service part A component to be sold by itself, in addition to being used in production to make a higher-level product. It is also referred to as a spare or a repair part. May be planned by MPSP or MRP.

Shipping date The date that the item is to ship to the customer. This is not the booking date, which is when the customer placed the order.

Shop order release A manufacturing function that controls when shop (work) orders should be released to the shop floor. Interfaces to PM & C to maintain actual shop floor activity. Also interfaces to MRP to keep the system updated on order status.

SOR See **Shop order release.**

Spare See **Service part.**

Statistical forecasting See **Forecasting.**

Statistical projections See **Forecasting.**

Stores control A manufacturing function which manages all of the data regarding how and where items are stocked/stored.

Structure data A bill of material or product structure which reflects a relationship of components to an end item or the relationship of items to a family.

Terminal A computer device at the end of a cable or telephone line that can input or access data from the computer's files.

Top management The management that is not concerned with day-to-day operations, but rather with long-range estimates of demand and production. Sets and manages the company direction. Performs business planning.

UM See **Unit of measure.**

Unit of measure The quantity by which production/sales/inventory is measured, such as gallons, square feet, and so on.

User A vague term. The term used to refer to anyone who was not associated with data processing and who used the data processing applications. Now since anyone can create and use manufacturing applications, the term has lost meaning. However, it still seems to mean non-data processing personnel in the majority of instances.

Variant A choice that *must* be selected as opposed to an option that *may* be selected. Variant mix percentages should add up to 100%. A variant on a car might be black (80%) or red (20%). A buyer has to pick a color (either black or red in this example). An option might be a radio (50%) or no radio.

A buyer does not have to select an option. Note that the term "option" often is applied to variants as well as to true options.

Weekly build schedule   Normally associated with a flow line or flow shop. Implies a rate per period, as X quantity per week. See **Flow line.**

Work center   A grouping of similar machines that have similar operational and overhead costs. Work centers may be grouped into major categories as cost centers.

Work center costs   The costs (in dollars) to process a part through the work center. Includes machine costs and various overhead costs.

APPENDIX IV

CONVERSION OF SALES DATA TO MANUFACTURING DATA

CONVERSION OF SALES DATA TO MANUFACTURING DATA FOR THE CHAPTER 3 MAKE-TO-STOCK AND PACKAGE-TO-ORDER COMPANY

Chapter Three developed projected model quantities by period. Figure 3.5 illustrated the mix percentages of the various product group as viewed by sales. Now each of these groups must be exploded by the indicated percentages.

The following tables illustrate the explosion to the end item levels for each of the families.

Product Group 602X Exploded to Price Groups

Period	Product Group Quantity	Price Groups and Percentages		
		A 24%	B 46%	C 30%
1	44,770	10,745	20,594	13,431
2	44,343	10,642	20,398	13,303
3	43,063	10,335	19,809	12,919
4	42,637	10,233	19,613	12,791
5	40,932	9,824	18,829	12,280
6	40,080	9,619	18,437	12,024
7	40,080	9,619	18,437	12,024
8	40,932	9,824	18,829	12,280
9	42,637	10,233	19,613	12,791
10	43,491	10,438	20,006	13,047
11	43,916	10,540	20,201	13,175
12	44,770	10,745	20,594	13,431

Each of the above three price groups must now be further exploded to end items.

Price Group A Exploded to End Items

Period	Price Group A Quantity	End Items and Percentages	
		602A 68%	602B 32%
1	10,745	7,307	3,438
2	10,642	7,237	3,405
3	10,335	7,028	3,307
4	10,233	6,958	3,275
5	9,824	6,680	3,144
6	9,619	6,541	3,078
7	9,619	6,541	3,078
8	9,824	6,680	3,144
9	10,233	6,958	3,275
10	10,438	7,098	3,340
11	10,540	7,167	3,373
12	10,745	7,307	3,438

Price Group B Exploded to End Items

Period	Price Group B Quantity	End Items and Percentages		
		602C 25%	602D 67%	602E 8%
1	20,594	5,149	13,798	1,648
2	20,398	5,100	13,667	1,632
3	19,809	4,952	13,272	1,585
4	19,613	4,903	13,141	1,569
5	18,829	4,707	12,615	1,506
6	18,437	4,609	12,353	1,475
7	18,437	4,609	12,353	1,475
8	18,829	4,707	12,615	1,506
9	19,613	4,903	13,141	1,569
10	20,006	5,002	13,404	1,600
11	20,201	5,050	13,535	1,616
12	20,594	5,149	13,798	1,648

Price Group C Exploded to End Items

Period	Price Group C Quantity	End Items and Percentages	
		602F 27%	602G 73%
1	13,431	3,626	9,805
2	13,303	3,592	9,711
3	12,919	3,488	9,431
4	12,791	3,454	9,337
5	12,280	3,316	8,964
6	12,024	3,246	8,778
7	12,024	3,246	8,778
8	12,280	3,316	8,964
9	12,791	3,454	9,337
10	13,047	3,523	9,524
11	13,175	3,557	9,618
12	13,431	3,626	9,805

The second product group was for product 502X. The explosion process is the same as for the previous group.

Product Group 502X Exploded to Price Groups

Period	Product Group Quantity	Price Groups and Percentages		
		D 22%	E 65%	F 13%
1	249,089	54,800	161,908	32,382
2	249,089	54,800	161,908	32,382
3	237,767	52,309	154,549	30,910
4	221,916	48,822	144,245	28,849
5	206,064	45,334	133,942	26,788
6	203,800	44,836	132,470	26,494
7	206,064	45,334	133,942	26,788
8	212,858	46,829	138,358	27,672
9	217,387	47,825	141,302	28,260
10	226,444	49,818	147,189	29,438
11	240,031	52,807	156,020	31,204
12	246,824	54,301	160,436	32,087

The three price groups are further exploded as shown below.

Price Group D Exploded to End Items

Period	Price Group D Quantity	End Items and Percentages		
		502A 20%	502B 40%	502C 40%
1	54,800	10,960	21,920	21,920
2	54,800	10,960	21,920	21,920
3	52,309	10,462	20,924	20,924
4	48,822	9,764	19,529	19,529
5	45,334	9,067	18,134	18,134
6	44,836	8,967	17,934	17,934
7	45,334	9,067	18,134	18,134
8	46,829	9,366	18,732	18,732
9	47,825	9,565	19,130	19,130
10	49,818	9,964	19,927	19,927
11	52,807	10,561	21,123	21,123
12	54,301	10,860	21,720	21,720

Price Group E Exploded to End Items

Period	Price Group E Quantity	End Items and Percentages 502D 36%	502E 64%
1	161,908	58,287	103,621
2	161,908	58,287	103,621
3	154,549	55,638	98,911
4	144,245	51,928	92,317
5	133,942	48,219	85,723
6	132,470	47,689	84,781
7	133,942	48,219	85,723
8	138,358	49,809	88,549
9	141,302	50,869	90,433
10	147,189	52,988	94,201
11	156,020	56,167	99,853
12	160,436	57,757	102,679

Price Group F Exploded to End Item

Period	Price Group F Quantity	End Item and Percentage 502F 100%
1	33,382	33,382
2	33,382	33,382
3	30,910	30,910
4	28,849	28,849
5	26,788	26,788
6	26,494	26,494
7	26,788	26,788
8	27,672	27,672
9	28,260	28,260
10	29,438	29,438
11	31,204	31,204
12	32,087	32,087

Product Group 840X Exploded to Price Group G and End Items

Period	Product Group Quantity	Price (100%) Group G Quantity	End Items and Percentages 840A 60%	840B 40%
1	1,047	1,047	628	419
2	1,057	1,057	634	423
3	1,057	1,057	634	423
4	1,069	1,069	641	428
5	1,080	1,080	648	432
6	1,111	1,111	667	444
7	1,100	1,100	660	440
8	1,080	1,080	648	432
9	1,069	1,069	641	428
10	1,057	1,057	634	423
11	1,047	1,047	628	419
12	1,047	1,047	628	419

CONVERSION OF SALES DATA TO MANUFACTURING DATA FOR THE CHAPTER 4 MAKE-TO-ORDER COMPANY

The first step performed by Manufacturing is to disaggregate the projected model quantities to option levels.

Figure A4.1 is an option planning product structure for the Model 901. A level-by-level percentage explosion of this structure is shown below.

Model 901 Level 0 to 1 Explosion

Level	Item	Mix Percentage	Monthly Period 1	2	3	4	5	6	7	8	9	10	11	12
0	901		6	8	10	16	6	6	6	5	5	5	6	6
1	RG901	100	6	8	10	16	6	6	6	5	5	5	6	6
1	PO33-901	100	6	8	10	16	6	6	6	5	5	5	6	6
1	PO45-901	100	6	8	10	16	6	6	6	5	5	5	6	6
1	PO51-901	100	6	8	10	16	6	6	6	5	5	5	6	6
1	PO65-901	100	6	8	10	16	6	6	6	5	5	5	6	6
1	PO68-901	100	6	8	10	16	6	6	6	5	5	5	6	6

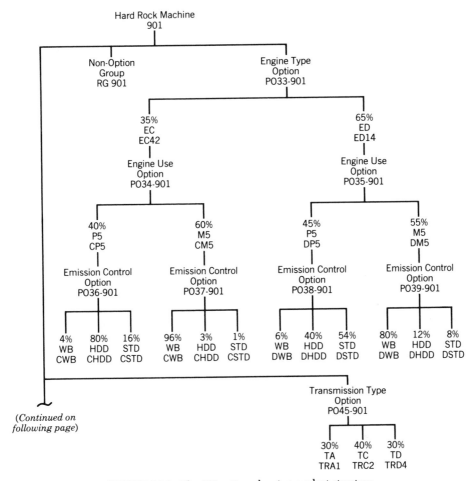

Hard Rock Machine
901

Non-Option
Group
RG 901

Engine Type
Option
PO33-901

35%
EC
EC42

65%
ED
ED14

Engine Use
Option
PO34-901

Engine Use
Option
PO35-901

40%
P5
CP5

60%
M5
CM5

45%
P5
DP5

55%
M5
DM5

Emission Control
Option
PO36-901

Emission Control
Option
PO37-901

Emission Control
Option
PO38-901

Emission Control
Option
PO39-901

4%	80%	16%	96%	3%	1%	6%	40%	54%	80%	12%	8%
WB	HDD	STD	WB	HDD	STD	WB	HDD	STD	WB	HDD	STD
CWB	CHDD	CSTD	CWB	CHDD	CSTD	DWB	DHDD	DSTD	DWB	DHDD	DSTD

Transmission Type
Option
PO45-901

(Continued on
following page)

30%	40%	30%
TA	TC	TD
TRA1	TRC2	TRD4

FIGURE A4.1 The 901 option planning product structure.

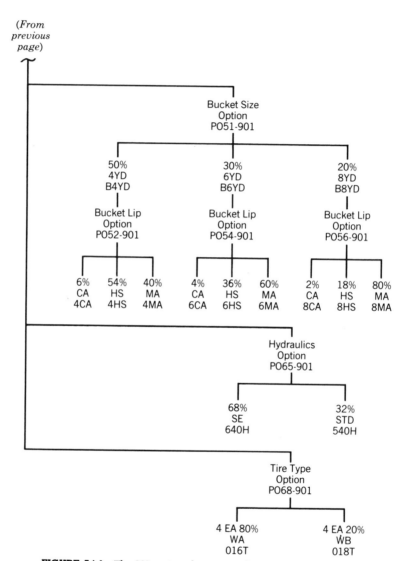

FIGURE A4.1 The 901 option planning product structure—Continued.

Model 901 Level 1 to 2 Explosion

Level	Item	Mix Percentage	Monthly Period											
			1	2	3	4	5	6	7	8	9	10	11	12
1	PO33-901		6	8	10	16	6	6	6	5	5	5	6	6
2	EC42	35	2	3	4	6	2	2	2	2	2	2	2	2
2	ED14	65	4	5	7	10	4	4	4	3	3	3	4	4
1	PO45-901		6	8	10	16	6	6	6	5	5	5	6	6
2	TRA1	30	2	2	3	5	2	2	2	2	2	2	2	2
2	TRC2	40	2	3	4	6	2	2	2	2	2	2	2	2
2	TRD4	30	2	2	3	5	2	2	2	2	2	2	2	2

At this point, if you are following the arithmetic, you will have noticed that rounding errors can be substantial. In actual practice, decimal positions may be utilized depending on the desired degree of accuracy. Normally, however, at the very general planning level, rounding errors do not have a significant impact on the final plan, unless the quantities per period are very small.

Model 901 Level 1 to 2 Explosion (Continued)

Level	Item	Mix Percentage	Monthly Period											
			1	2	3	4	5	6	7	8	9	10	11	12
1	PO51-901		6	8	10	16	6	6	6	5	5	5	6	6
2	B4YD	50	3	4	5	8	3	3	3	3	3	3	3	3
2	B6YD	30	2	2	3	5	2	2	2	2	2	2	2	2
2	B8YD	20	1	2	3	1	1	1	1	1	1	1	1	1
1	PO65-901		6	8	10	16	6	6	6	5	5	5	6	6
2	640H	68	4	5	7	11	4	4	4	3	3	3	4	4
2	540H	32	2	3	3	5	2	2	2	2	2	2	2	2
1	PO68-901		6	8	10	16	6	6	6	5	5	5	6	6
2	016T	80	19	26	32	51	19	19	19	16	16	16	19	19
2	018T	20	5	6	8	13	5	5	5	4	4	4	5	5

Note that when PO68-901 is exploded, the resultant quantity must be extended by a quantity of four, as four each are required (such as 4 each 016Ts) for every PO68-901.

Model 901 Level 2 to 3 Explosion

Level	Item	Mix Percentage	Monthly Period											
			1	2	3	4	5	6	7	8	9	10	11	12
2	EC42		2	3	4	6	2	2	2	2	2	2	2	2
3	CP5	40	1	1	2	2	1	1	1	1	1	1	1	1
3	CM5	60	1	2	2	4	1	1	1	1	1	1	1	1
2	ED14		4	5	7	10	4	4	4	3	3	3	4	4
3	DP5	45	2	2	3	5	2	2	2	1	1	1	2	2
3	DM5	55	2	3	4	6	2	2	2	2	2	2	2	2
2	B4YD		3	4	5	8	3	3	3	3	3	3	3	3
3	4CA	6	0	0	0	0	0	0	0	0	0	0	0	0
3	4HS	54	2	2	3	4	2	2	2	2	2	2	2	2
3	4MA	40	1	2	2	3	1	1	1	1	1	1	1	1
2	B6YD		2	2	3	5	2	2	2	2	2	2	2	2
3	6CA	4	0	0	0	0	0	0	0	0	0	0	0	0
3	6HS	36	1	1	1	2	1	1	1	1	1	1	1	1
3	6MA	60	1	1	2	3	1	1	1	1	1	1	1	1
2	B8YD		1	2	2	3	1	1	1	1	1	1	1	1
3	8CA	2	4	0	0	0	0	0	0	0	0	0	0	0
3	8HS	18	0	0	0	1	0	0	0	0	0	0	0	0
3	8MA	80	1	2	2	2	1	1	1	1	1	1	1	1

Model 901 Level 3 to 4 Explosion

Level	Item	Mix Percentage	Monthly Period											
			1	2	3	4	5	6	7	8	9	10	11	12
3	CP5		1	1	2	2	1	1	1	1	1	1	1	1
4	CWB	4	0	0	0	0	0	0	0	0	0	0	0	0
4	CHDD	80	1	1	2	2	1	1	1	1	1	1	1	1
4	CSTD	16	0	0	0	0	0	0	0	0	0	0	0	0
3	CM5		1	2	2	4	1	1	1	1	1	1	1	1
4	CWB	96	1	2	2	4	1	1	1	1	1	1	1	1
4	CHDD	3	0	0	0	0	0	0	0	0	0	0	0	0
4	CSTD	1	0	0	0	0	0	0	0	0	0	0	0	0
3	DP5		2	2	3	5	2	2	2	1	1	1	2	2
4	DWB	6	0	0	0	0	0	0	0	0	0	0	0	0
4	DHDD	40	1	1	1	2	1	1	1	0	0	0	1	1
4	DSTD	54	1	1	2	3	1	1	1	1	1	1	1	1
3	DM5		2	3	4	6	2	2	2	2	2	2	2	2
4	DWB	80	2	2	3	5	2	2	2	2	2	2	2	2
4	DHDD	12	0	0	0	1	0	0	0	0	0	0	0	0
4	DSTD	8	0	0	0	0	0	0	0	0	0	0	0	0

Figure A4.2 is the option planning product structure for Model 902. The level-by-level explosion is shown on the following pages.

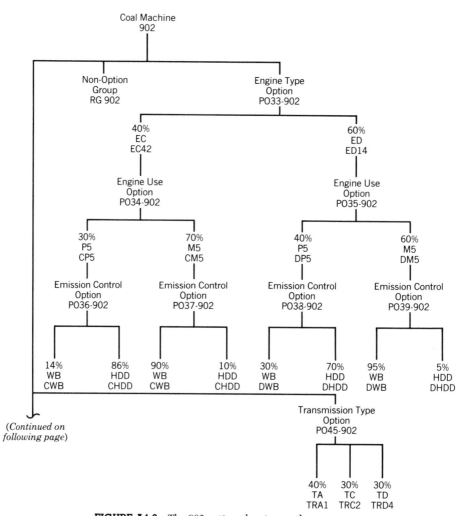

(Continued on
following page)

FIGURE A4.2   The 902 option planning product structure.

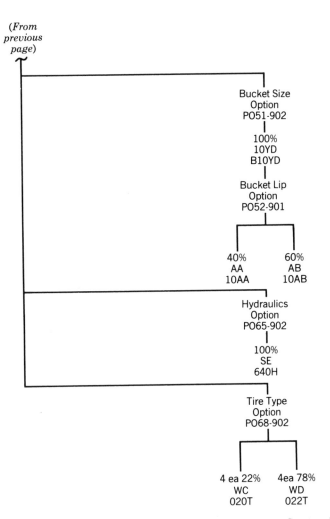

FIGURE A4.2 The 902 option planning product structure—Continued.

Model 902 Level 0 to 1 Explosion

Level	Item	Mix Percentage	Monthly Period											
			1	2	3	4	5	6	7	8	9	10	11	12
0	902		40	40	40	40	40	40	40	40	40	40	40	40
1	RG902	100	40	40	40	40	40	40	40	40	40	40	40	40
1	PO33-902	100	40	40	40	40	40	40	40	40	40	40	40	40
1	PO45-902	100	40	40	40	40	40	40	40	40	40	40	40	40
1	PO51-902	100	40	40	40	40	40	40	40	40	40	40	40	40
1	PO65-902	100	40	40	40	40	40	40	40	40	40	40	40	40
1	PO68-902	100	40	40	40	40	40	40	40	40	40	40	40	40

Model 902 Level 1 to 2 Explosion

Level	Item	Mix Percentage	Monthly Period											
			1	2	3	4	5	6	7	8	9	10	11	12
1	PO33-902		40	40	40	40	40	40	40	40	40	40	40	40
2	EC42	40	16	16	16	16	16	16	16	16	16	16	16	16
2	ED14	60	24	24	24	24	24	24	24	24	24	24	24	24
1	PO45-902	40	40	40	40	40	40	40	40	40	40	40	40	40
2	TRA1	40	16	16	16	16	16	16	16	16	16	16	16	16
2	TRC2	30	12	12	12	12	12	12	12	12	12	12	12	12
2	TRD4	30	12	12	12	12	12	12	12	12	12	12	12	12
1	PO51-902		40	40	40	40	40	40	40	40	40	40	40	40
2	B10YD	100	40	40	40	40	40	40	40	40	40	40	40	40
1	PO65-902		40	40	40	40	40	40	40	40	40	40	40	40
2	640H	100	40	40	40	40	40	40	40	40	40	40	40	40
1	PO68-902		40	40	40	40	40	40	40	40	40	40	40	40
2	020T	22	35	35	35	35	35	35	35	35	35	35	35	35
2	022T	78	125	125	125	125	125	125	125	125	125	125	125	125

Model 902 Level 2 to 3 Explosion

Level	Item	Mix Percentage	Monthly Period											
			1	2	3	4	5	6	7	8	9	10	11	12
2	EC42		16	16	16	16	16	16	16	16	16	16	16	16
3	CP5	30	5	5	5	5	5	5	5	5	5	5	5	5
3	CM5	70	11	11	11	11	11	11	11	11	11	11	11	11
2	ED14		24	24	24	24	24	24	24	24	24	24	24	24
3	DP5	40	10	10	10	10	10	10	10	10	10	10	10	10
3	DM5	60	14	14	14	14	14	14	14	14	14	14	14	14
2	B10YD		40	40	40	40	40	40	40	40	40	40	40	40
3	10AA	40	16	16	16	16	16	16	16	16	16	16	16	16
3	10AB	60	24	24	24	24	24	24	24	24	24	24	24	24

Model 902 Level 3 to 4 Explosion

Level	Item	Mix Percentage	Monthly Period											
			1	2	3	4	5	6	7	8	9	10	11	12
3	CP5		5	5	5	5	5	5	5	5	5	5	5	5
4	CWB	14	1	1	1	1	1	1	1	1	1	1	1	1
4	CHDD	86	4	4	4	4	4	4	4	4	4	4	4	4
3	CM5		11	11	11	11	11	11	11	11	11	11	11	11
4	CWB	90	10	10	10	10	10	10	10	10	10	10	10	10
4	CHDD	10	1	1	1	1	1	1	1	1	1	1	1	1
3	DP5		10	10	10	10	10	10	10	10	10	10	10	10
4	DWB	30	3	3	3	3	3	3	3	3	3	3	3	3
4	DHDD	70	7	7	7	7	7	7	7	7	7	7	7	7
3	DM5		14	14	14	14	14	14	14	14	14	14	14	14
4	DWB	95	13	13	13	13	13	13	13	13	13	13	13	13
4	DHDD	5	1	1	1	1	1	1	1	1	1	1	1	1

Figure A4.3 is the option planning product structure for Model 905. The level-by-level explosion is shown on the following pages.

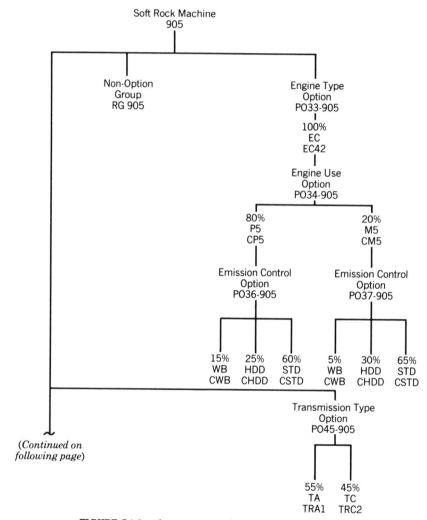

(*Continued on
following page*)

FIGURE A4.3 The 905 option planning product structure.

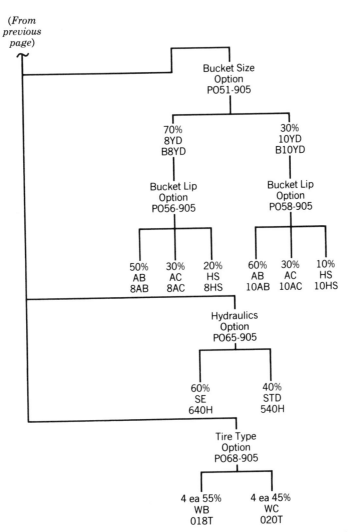

FIGURE A4.3 The 905 option planning product structure—Continued.

Model 905 Level 0 to 1 Explosion

Level	Item	Mix Percentage	Monthly Period											
			1	2	3	4	5	6	7	8	9	10	11	12
0	905		5	4	3	2	1	0	0	0	0	0	0	0
1	RG905	100	5	4	3	2	1	0	0	0	0	0	0	0
1	PO33-905	100	5	4	3	2	1	0	0	0	0	0	0	0
1	PO45-905	100	5	4	3	2	1	0	0	0	0	0	0	0
1	PO51-905	100	5	4	3	2	1	0	0	0	0	0	0	0
1	PO65-905	100	5	4	3	2	1	0	0	0	0	0	0	0
1	PO68-905	100	5	4	3	2	1	0	0	0	0	0	0	0

Model 905 Level 1 to 2 Explosion

Level	Item	Mix Percentage	Monthly Period											
			1	2	3	4	5	6	7	8	9	10	11	12
1	PO33-905		5	4	3	2	1	0	0	0	0	0	0	0
2	EC42	100	5	4	3	2	1	0	0	0	0	0	0	0
1	PO45-905		5	4	3	2	1	0	0	0	0	0	0	0
2	TRA1	55	3	2	2	1	1	0	0	0	0	0	0	0
2	TRC2	45	2	2	1	1	0	0	0	0	0	0	0	0
1	PO51-905		5	4	3	2	1	0	0	0	0	0	0	0
2	B8YD	70	4	3	2	1	1	0	0	0	0	0	0	0
2	B10YD	30	2	1	1	1	0	0	0	0	0	0	0	0
1	PO65-905		5	4	3	2	1	0	0	0	0	0	0	0
2	640H	60	3	2	2	1	1	0	0	0	0	0	0	0
2	540H	40	2	2	1	1	0	0	0	0	0	0	0	0
1	PO68-905		5	4	3	2	1	0	0	0	0	0	0	0
2	018T	55	11	9	7	4	2	0	0	0	0	0	0	0
2	020T	45	9	7	5	4	2	0	0	0	0	0	0	0

Model 905 Level 2 to 3 Explosion

Level	Item	Mix Percentage	Monthly Period											
			1	2	3	4	5	6	7	8	9	10	11	12
2	EC42		5	4	3	2	1	0	0	0	0	0	0	0
3	CP5	80	4	2	2	2	1	0	0	0	0	0	0	0
3	CM5	20	1	1	1	0	0	0	0	0	0	0	0	0
2	B8YD		4	3	2	1	1	0	0	0	0	0	0	0
3	8AB	50	2	2	1	1	1	0	0	0	0	0	0	0
3	8AC	30	1	1	1	0	0	0	0	0	0	0	0	0
3	8HS	20	1	1	0	0	0	0	0	0	0	0	0	0
2	B10YD		2	1	1	1	0	0	0	0	0	0	0	0
3	10AB	60	1	1	1	1	0	0	0	0	0	0	0	0
3	10AC	30	1	0	0	0	0	0	0	0	0	0	0	0
3	10HS	10	0	0	0	0	0	0	0	0	0	0	0	0

Model 905 Level 3 to 4 Explosion

Level	Item	Mix Percentage	Monthly Period											
			1	2	3	4	5	6	7	8	9	10	11	12
3	CP5		4	2	2	2	1	0	0	0	0	0	0	0
4	CWB	15	1	0	0	0	0	0	0	0	0	0	0	0
4	CHDD	25	1	1	1	1	0	0	0	0	0	0	0	0
4	CSTD	60	2	1	1	1	1	0	0	0	0	0	0	0
3	CM5		1	1	1	0	0	0	0	0	0	0	0	0
4	CWB	5	0	0	0	0	0	0	0	0	0	0	0	0
4	CHDD	30	0	0	0	0	0	0	0	0	0	0	0	0
4	CSTD	65	1	1	1	0	0	0	0	0	0	0	0	0

Figure A4.4 is the option planning structure for Model 910. The level-by-level explosion is shown on the following pages.

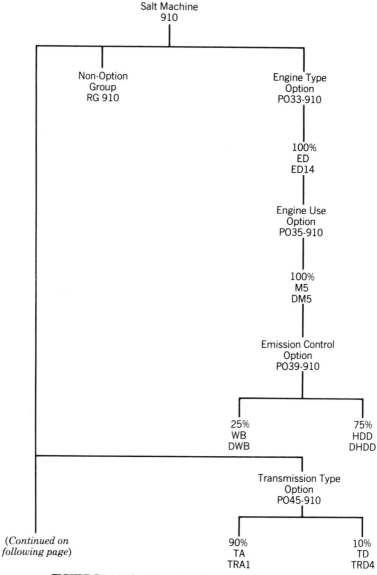

(*Continued on*
following page)

FIGURE A4.4   The 910 option planning product structure.

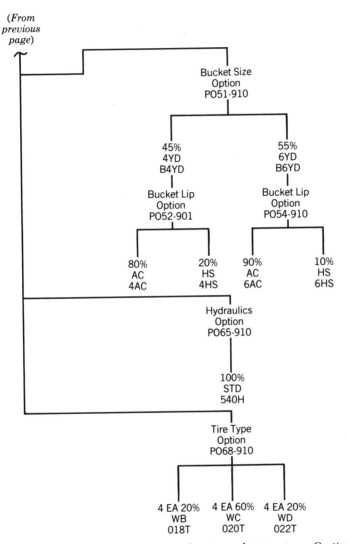

FIGURE A4.4 The 910 option planning product structure—Continued.

Model 910 Level 0 to 1 Explosion

Level	Item	Mix Percentage	Monthly Period											
			1	2	3	4	5	6	7	8	9	10	11	12
0	910		0	1	2	3	4	5	6	7	8	8	8	8
1	RG910	100	0	1	2	3	4	5	6	7	8	8	8	8
1	PO33-910	100	0	1	2	3	4	5	6	7	8	8	8	8
1	PO45-910	100	0	1	2	3	4	5	6	7	8	8	8	8
1	PO51-910	100	0	1	2	3	4	5	6	7	8	8	8	8
1	PO65-910	100	0	1	2	3	4	5	6	7	8	8	8	8
1	PO68-910	100	0	1	2	3	4	5	6	7	8	8	8	8

Model 910 Level 1 to 2 Explosion

Level	Item	Mix Percentage	Monthly Period											
			1	2	3	4	5	6	7	8	9	10	11	12
1	PO33-901		0	1	2	3	4	5	6	7	8	8	8	8
2	ED14	100	0	1	2	3	4	5	6	7	8	8	8	8
1	PO45-910		0	1	2	3	4	5	6	7	8	8	8	8
2	TRA1	90	0	1	2	2	4	5	5	6	7	7	7	7
2	TRD4	10	0	0	0	0	0	1	1	1	1	1	1	1
1	PO51-910		0	1	2	3	4	5	6	7	8	8	8	8
2	B4YD	45	0	0	1	1	2	2	3	3	4	4	4	4
2	B6YD	55	0	1	1	2	2	3	3	4	4	4	4	4
1	PO65-910		0	1	2	3	4	5	6	7	8	8	8	8
2	540H	100	0	1	2	3	4	5	6	7	8	8	8	8
1	PO68-910		0	1	2	3	4	5	6	7	8	8	8	8
2	018T	20	0	1	2	2	3	4	5	7	8	8	8	8
2	020T	60	0	2	5	7	10	12	14	17	19	19	19	19
2	022T	20	0	1	2	2	3	4	5	7	8	8	8	8

Model 910 Level 2 to 3 Explosion

Level	Item	Mix Percentage	Monthly Period											
			1	2	3	4	5	6	7	8	9	10	11	12
2	ED14		0	1	2	3	4	5	6	7	8	8	8	8
3	DM5	100	0	1	2	3	4	5	6	7	8	8	8	8
2	B4YD		0	0	1	1	2	2	3	3	4	4	4	4
3	4AC	80	0	0	1	1	2	2	2	2	3	3	3	3
3	4HS	20	0	0	0	0	0	0	1	1	1	1	1	1
2	B6YD		0	1	1	2	2	3	3	4	4	4	4	4
3	6AC	90	0	1	1	2	2	2	2	3	3	3	3	3
3	6HS	10	0	0	0	0	0	0	0	0	0	0	0	0

Model 910 Level 3 to 4 Explosion

Level	Item	Mix Percentage	Monthly Period											
			1	2	3	4	5	6	7	8	9	10	11	12
3	DM5		0	1	2	3	4	5	6	7	8	8	8	8
4	DWB	25	0	0	1	1	1	1	2	2	2	2	2	2
4	DHDD	75	0	1	2	2	3	4	5	5	6	6	6	6

A clearer picture of the option requirements (forecasts) by model is shown below with a summarization of the explosion data. Note that a line of dashes by a machine type indicates that that option was not available (applicable) for that machine.

Machine	Item	Monthly Period											
		1	2	3	4	5	6	7	8	9	10	11	12
Non-Option Groups													
901	RG901	6	8	10	16	6	6	6	5	5	5	6	6
902	RG902	40	40	40	40	40	40	40	40	40	40	40	40
905	RG905	5	4	3	2	1	0	0	0	0	0	0	0
910	RG910	0	1	2	3	4	5	6	7	8	8	8	8
Engines													
901	EC42	2	3	4	6	2	2	2	2	2	2	2	2
902		16	16	16	16	16	16	16	16	16	16	16	16
905		5	4	3	2	1	0	0	0	0	0	0	0
910		—	—	—	—	—	—	—	—	—	—	—	—
Total		23	23	23	24	19	18	18	18	18	18	18	18
Engines													
901	ED14	4	5	7	10	4	4	4	3	3	3	4	4
902		24	24	24	24	24	24	24	24	24	24	24	24
905		—	—	—	—	—	—	—	—	—	—	—	—
910		0	1	2	3	4	5	6	7	8	8	8	8
Total		28	30	33	37	32	33	34	34	35	35	36	36
Engine Altitude Usage Kits													
901	CP5	1	1	2	2	1	1	1	1	1	1	1	1
902		5	5	5	5	5	5	5	5	5	5	5	5
905		4	2	2	2	1	0	0	0	0	0	0	0
910		—	—	—	—	—	—	—	—	—	—	—	—
Total		10	8	9	9	7	6	6	6	6	6	6	6

(*continued*)

		Monthly Period											
Machine	Item	1	2	3	4	5	6	7	8	9	10	11	12

Engine Altitude Usage Kits

Machine	Item	1	2	3	4	5	6	7	8	9	10	11	12
901	CM5	1	2	2	4	1	1	1	1	1	1	1	1
902		11	11	11	11	11	11	11	11	11	11	11	11
905		1	1	1	0	0	0	0	0	0	0	0	0
910		—	—	—	—	—	—	—	—	—	—	—	—
Total		13	14	14	15	12	12	12	12	12	12	12	12

Engine Altitude Usage Kits

Machine	Item	1	2	3	4	5	6	7	8	9	10	11	12
901	DP5	2	2	3	5	2	2	2	1	1	1	2	2
902		10	10	10	10	10	10	10	10	10	10	10	10
905		—	—	—	—	—	—	—	—	—	—	—	—
910		—	—	—	—	—	—	—	—	—	—	—	—
Total		12	12	13	15	12	12	12	11	11	11	12	12

Engine Altitude Usage Kits

Machine	Item	1	2	3	4	5	6	7	8	9	10	11	12
901	DM5	2	3	4	6	2	2	2	2	2	2	2	2
902		14	14	14	14	14	14	14	14	14	14	14	14
905		—	—	—	—	—	—	—	—	—	—	—	—
910		0	1	2	3	4	5	6	7	8	8	8	8
Total		16	18	20	23	20	21	22	23	24	24	24	24

Emission Control Kits

Machine	Item	1	2	3	4	5	6	7	8	9	10	11	12
901	CWB	1	2	2	4	1	1	1	1	1	1	1	1
902		11	11	11	11	11	11	11	11	11	11	11	11
905		1	0	0	0	0	0	0	0	0	0	0	0
910		—	—	—	—	—	—	—	—	—	—	—	—
Total		13	13	13	15	12	12	12	12	12	12	12	12

Emission Control Kits

Machine	Item	1	2	3	4	5	6	7	8	9	10	11	12
901	CHDD	1	1	2	2	1	1	1	1	1	1	1	1
902		5	5	5	5	5	5	5	5	5	5	5	5
905		1	1	1	1	0	0	0	0	0	0	0	0
910		—	—	—	—	—	—	—	—	—	—	—	—
Total		7	7	8	8	6	6	6	6	6	6	6	6

(*continued*)

Machine	Item	Monthly Period											
		1	2	3	4	5	6	7	8	9	10	11	12
Emission Control Kits													
901	CSTD	0	0	0	0	0	0	0	0	0	0	0	0
902		—	—	—	—	—	—	—	—	—	—	—	—
905		3	2	2	1	1	0	0	0	0	0	0	0
910		—	—	—	—	—	—	—	—	—	—	—	—
Total		3	2	2	1	1	1	0	0	0	0	0	0
Emission Control Kits													
901	DWB	2	2	3	5	2	2	2	2	2	2	2	2
902		16	16	16	16	16	16	16	16	16	16	16	16
905		—	—	—	—	—	—	—	—	—	—	—	—
910		0	0	1	1	1	1	2	2	2	2	2	2
Total		18	18	19	21	18	18	18	18	18	18	18	18
Emission Control Kits													
901	DHDD	1	1	1	3	1	1	1	0	0	0	1	1
902		8	8	8	8	8	8	8	8	8	8	8	8
905		—	—	—	—	—	—	—	—	—	—	—	—
910		0	1	2	2	3	4	5	5	6	6	6	6
Total		9	9	9	11	9	9	9	8	8	8	9	9
Emission Control Kits													
901	DSTD	1	1	2	3	1	1	1	1	1	1	1	1
902		—	—	—	—	—	—	—	—	—	—	—	—
905		—	—	—	—	—	—	—	—	—	—	—	—
910		—	—	—	—	—	—	—	—	—	—	—	—
Total		1	1	2	3	1	1	1	1	1	1	1	1
Transmissions													
901	TRA1	2	2	3	5	2	2	2	2	2	2	2	2
902		16	16	16	16	16	16	16	16	16	16	16	16
905		3	2	2	1	1	0	0	0	0	0	0	0
910		0	1	2	2	4	5	5	6	7	7	7	7
Total		21	21	23	24	23	23	23	24	25	25	25	25

(continued)

		Monthly Period											
Machine	Item	1	2	3	4	5	6	7	8	9	10	11	12
Transmissions													
901	TRC2	2	3	4	6	2	2	2	2	2	2	2	2
902		12	12	12	12	12	12	12	12	12	12	12	12
905		2	2	1	1	0	0	0	0	0	0	0	0
910		—	—	—	—	—	—	—	—	—	—	—	—
Total		16	17	17	19	14	14	14	14	14	14	14	14
Transmissions													
901	TRD4	2	2	3	5	2	2	2	2	2	2	2	2
902		12	12	12	12	12	12	12	12	12	12	12	12
905		—	—	—	—	—	—	—	—	—	—	—	—
910		0	0	0	0	0	1	1	1	1	1	1	1
Total		14	14	15	17	14	14	14	14	14	14	14	14
Buckets													
901	B4YD	3	4	5	8	3	3	3	3	3	3	3	3
902		—	—	—	—	—	—	—	—	—	—	—	—
905		—	—	—	—	—	—	—	—	—	—	—	—
910		0	0	1	1	2	2	3	3	4	4	4	4
Total		3	4	6	9	5	5	6	6	7	7	7	7
Buckets													
901	B6YD	2	2	3	5	2	2	2	2	2	2	2	2
902		—	—	—	—	—	—	—	—	—	—	—	—
905		—	—	—	—	—	—	—	—	—	—	—	—
910		0	1	1	2	2	3	3	4	4	4	4	4
Total		2	3	4	7	4	5	5	6	6	6	6	6
Buckets													
901	B8YD	1	2	2	3	1	1	1	1	1	1	1	1
902		—	—	—	—	—	—	—	—	—	—	—	—
905		4	3	2	1	1	0	0	0	0	0	0	0
910		—	—	—	—	—	—	—	—	—	—	—	—
Total		5	5	4	4	2	1	1	1	1	1	1	1

(*continued*)

							Monthly Period						
Machine	Item	1	2	3	4	5	6	7	8	9	10	11	12

Buckets

901	B10YD	—	—	—	—	—	—	—	—	—	—	—	—
902		40	40	40	40	40	40	40	40	40	40	40	40
905		2	1	1	1	0	0	0	0	0	0	0	0
910		—	—	—	—	—	—	—	—	—	—	—	—
Total		42	41	41	41	40	40	40	40	40	40	40	40

Bucket Lips

901	4AC	—	—	—	—	—	—	—	—	—	—	—	—
902		—	—	—	—	—	—	—	—	—	—	—	—
905		—	—	—	—	—	—	—	—	—	—	—	—
910		0	0	1	1	2	2	2	2	3	3	3	3
Total		0	0	1	1	2	2	2	2	3	3	3	3

Bucket Lips

901	4CA	0	0	0	0	0	0	0	0	0	0	0	0
902		—	—	—	—	—	—	—	—	—	—	—	—
905		—	—	—	—	—	—	—	—	—	—	—	—
910		—	—	—	—	—	—	—	—	—	—	—	—
Total		0	0	0	0	0	0	0	0	0	0	0	0

Bucket Lips

901	4HS	2	2	3	4	2	2	2	2	2	2	2	2
902		—	—	—	—	—	—	—	—	—	—	—	—
905		—	—	—	—	—	—	—	—	—	—	—	—
910		0	0	0	0	0	0	1	1	1	1	1	1
Total		2	2	3	4	2	2	2	3	3	3	3	3

Bucket Lips

901	4MA	1	2	2	3	1	1	1	1	1	1	1	1
902		—	—	—	—	—	—	—	—	—	—	—	—
905		—	—	—	—	—	—	—	—	—	—	—	—
910		—	—	—	—	—	—	—	—	—	—	—	—
Total		1	2	2	3	1	1	1	1	1	1	1	1

(continued)

		Monthly Period											
Machine	Item	1	2	3	4	5	6	7	8	9	10	11	12
Bucket Lips													
901	6AC	—	—	—	—	—	—	—	—	—	—	—	—
902		—	—	—	—	—	—	—	—	—	—	—	—
905		—	—	—	—	—	—	—	—	—	—	—	—
910		0	1	1	2	2	2	2	3	3	3	3	3
Total		0	1	1	2	2	2	2	3	3	3	3	3
Bucket Lips													
901	6CA	0	0	0	0	0	0	0	0	0	0	0	0
902		—	—	—	—	—	—	—	—	—	—	—	—
905		—	—	—	—	—	—	—	—	—	—	—	—
910		—	—	—	—	—	—	—	—	—	—	—	—
Total		0	0	0	0	0	0	0	0	0	0	0	0
Bucket Lips													
901	6HS	1	1	1	2	1	1	1	1	1	1	1	1
902		—	—	—	—	—	—	—	—	—	—	—	—
905		—	—	—	—	—	—	—	—	—	—	—	—
910		0	0	0	0	0	0	0	0	0	0	0	0
Total		1	1	1	2	1	1	1	1	1	1	1	1
Bucket Lips													
901	6MA	1	1	2	3	1	1	1	1	1	1	1	1
902		—	—	—	—	—	—	—	—	—	—	—	—
905		—	—	—	—	—	—	—	—	—	—	—	—
910		—	—	—	—	—	—	—	—	—	—	—	—
Total		1	1	2	3	1	1	1	1	1	1	1	1
Bucket Lips													
901	8AB	—	—	—	—	—	—	—	—	—	—	—	—
902		—	—	—	—	—	—	—	—	—	—	—	—
905		2	2	1	1	1	0	0	0	0	0	0	0
910		—	—	—	—	—	—	—	—	—	—	—	—
Total		2	2	1	1	1	0	0	0	0	0	0	0

(*continued*)

		Monthly Period											
Machine	Item	1	2	3	4	5	6	7	8	9	10	11	12
Bucket Lips													
901	8AC	—	—	—	—	—	—	—	—	—	—	—	—
902		—	—	—	—	—	—	—	—	—	—	—	—
905		1	1	1	0	0	0	0	0	0	0	0	0
910		—	—	—	—	—	—	—	—	—	—	—	—
Total		1	1	1	0	0	0	0	0	0	0	0	0
Bucket Lips													
901	8CA	0	0	0	0	0	0	0	0	0	0	0	0
902		—	—	—	—	—	—	—	—	—	—	—	—
905		—	—	—	—	—	—	—	—	—	—	—	—
910		—	—	—	—	—	—	—	—	—	—	—	—
Total		0	0	0	0	0	0	0	0	0	0	0	0
Bucket Lips													
901	8HS	0	0	0	1	0	0	0	0	0	0	0	0
902		—	—	—	—	—	—	—	—	—	—	—	—
905		1	1	0	0	0	0	0	0	0	0	0	0
910		—	—	—	—	—	—	—	—	—	—	—	—
Total		1	1	0	1	0	0	0	0	0	0	0	
Bucket Lips													
901	8MA	1	2	2	2	1	1	1	1	1	1	1	1
902		—	—	—	—	—	—	—	—	—	—	—	—
905		—	—	—	—	—	—	—	—	—	—	—	—
910		—	—	—	—	—	—	—	—	—	—	—	—
Total		1	2	2	2	1	1	1	1	1	1	1	1
Bucket Lips													
901	10AA	—	—	—	—	—	—	—	—	—	—	1	1
902		16	16	16	16	16	16	16	16	16	16	16	16
905		—	—	—	—	—	—	—	—	—	—	—	—
910		—	—	—	—	—	—	—	—	—	—	—	—
Total		16	16	16	16	16	16	16	16	16	16	16	16

(continued)

Machine	Item	Monthly Period											
		1	2	3	4	5	6	7	8	9	10	11	12
Bucket Lips													
901	10AB	—	—	—	—	—	—	—	—	—	—	—	—
902		24	24	24	24	24	24	24	24	24	24	24	24
905		1	1	1	1	0	0	0	0	0	0	0	0
910		—	—	—	—	—	—	—	—	—	—	—	—
Total		25	25	25	25	24	24	24	24	24	24	24	24
Bucket Lips													
901	10AC	—	—	—	—	—	—	—	—	—	—	—	—
902		—	—	—	—	—	—	—	—	—	—	—	—
905		1	0	0	0	0	0	0	0	0	0	0	0
910		—	—	—	—	—	—	—	—	—	—	—	—
Total		1	0	0	0	0	0	0	0	0	0	0	0
Bucket Lips													
901	10HS	—	—	—	—	—	—	—	—	—	—	—	—
902		—	—	—	—	—	—	—	—	—	—	—	—
905		0	0	0	0	0	0	0	0	0	0	0	0
910		—	—	—	—	—	—	—	—	—	—	—	—
Total		0	0	0	0	0	0	0	0	0	0	0	0
Hydraulic Kits													
901	640H	4	5	7	11	4	4	4	3	3	3	4	4
902		40	40	40	40	40	40	40	40	40	40	40	40
905		3	2	2	1	1	0	0	0	0	0	0	0
910		—	—	—	—	—	—	—	—	—	—	—	—
Total		47	47	49	52	45	44	44	43	43	43	44	44
Hydraulic Kits													
901	540H	2	3	3	5	2	2	2	2	2	2	2	2
902		—	—	—	—	—	—	—	—	—	—	—	—
905		2	2	1	1	0	0	0	0	0	0	0	0
910		0	1	2	3	4	5	6	7	8	8	8	8
Total		4	6	6	9	6	7	8	9	10	10	10	10

(continued)

Machine	Item	Monthly Period											
		1	2	3	4	5	6	7	8	9	10	11	12
Tires													
901	016T	19	26	32	51	19	19	19	16	16	16	19	19
902		—	—	—	—	—	—	—	—	—	—	—	—
905		—	—	—	—	—	—	—	—	—	—	—	—
910		—	—	—	—	—	—	—	—	—	—	—	—
Total		19	26	32	51	19	19	19	16	16	16	19	19
Tires													
901	018T	5	6	8	13	5	5	5	4	4	4	5	5
902		—	—	—	—	—	—	—	—	—	—	—	—
905		11	9	7	4	2	0	0	0	0	0	0	0
910		0	1	2	2	3	4	5	7	8	8	8	8
Total		16	16	17	19	10	9	10	11	12	12	13	13
Tires													
901	020T	—	—	—	—	—	—	—	—	—	—	—	—
902		35	35	35	35	35	35	35	35	35	35	35	35
905		9	7	5	4	2	0	0	0	0	0	0	0
910		0	2	5	7	10	12	14	17	19	19	19	19
Total		44	44	45	46	47	47	49	52	54	54	54	54
Tires													
901	022T	—	—	—	—	—	—	—	—	—	—	—	—
902		125	125	125	125	125	125	125	125	125	125	125	125
905		—	—	—	—	—	—	—	—	—	—	—	—
910		0	1	2	2	3	4	5	7	8	8	8	8
Total		125	126	127	127	128	129	130	132	133	133	133	133

As mentioned earlier, buckets and bucket lips are also sold as service or replacement parts. This service part forecast has been accumulated from service/repair facilities that handle the maintenance of the machines. The total forecast (option and service) is described by the following calculations.

To keep the calculations simple, assume that no new lips are supplied with service buckets. Note that not all lips have service part demand.

(*continued*)

Item	Forecast	Monthly Period											
		1	2	3	4	5	6	7	8	9	10	11	12
Buckets													
B4YD	Option	3	4	6	9	5	5	6	6	7	7	7	7
	Service	0	1	0	1	1	2	2	1	1	2	2	3
Total		3	5	6	10	6	7	8	7	8	9	9	10
Buckets													
B6YD	Option	2	3	4	7	4	5	5	6	6	6	6	6
	Service	0	0	0	1	0	0	2	1	0	1	1	1
Total		2	3	4	8	4	5	7	7	6	7	7	7
Buckets													
B8YD	Option	5	5	4	4	2	1	1	1	1	1	1	1
	Service	3	2	1	0	1	0	2	1	2	1	0	1
Total		8	7	5	4	3	1	3	2	3	2	1	2
Buckets													
B10YD	Option	42	41	41	41	40	40	40	40	40	40	40	40
	Service	10	10	11	10	11	12	11	12	13	12	13	14
Total		52	51	52	51	51	52	51	52	53	52	53	54
Bucket Lips													
4HS	Option	2	2	4	4	2	2	3	3	3	3	3	3
	Service	0	0	0	0	0	1	2	0	0	1	1	1
Total		2	2	3	4	2	3	5	3	3	4	4	4
Bucket Lips													
6AC	Option	0	1	1	2	2	2	2	3	3	3	3	3
	Service	0	0	0	0	1	0	0	1	0	0	1	1
Total		0	1	1	2	3	2	2	4	3	3	4	4

(continued)

Item	Forecast	Monthly Period											
		1	2	3	4	5	6	7	8	9	10	11	12
Bucket Lips													
10AA	Option	16	16	16	16	16	16	16	16	16	16	16	16
	Service	4	5	4	4	5	5	6	5	6	6	7	6
Total		20	21	20	20	21	21	22	21	22	22	23	22
Bucket Lips													
10AB	Option	25	25	25	25	24	24	24	24	24	24	24	24
	Service	10	11	12	12	13	14	14	15	16	16	17	18
Total		35	36	37	37	37	38	38	39	40	40	41	42